CONSCIENCE

P. D. Ouspensky (1878–1947) was born in Moscow. His books *Tertium Organum* and *A New Model of the Universe* (Arkana, 1984) revealed his stature as a thinker and his deep preoccupation with the problems of man's existence. After his work with Gurdjieff between 1915 and 1918, his interest centred on the practical study of methods for the development of consciousness in man, as expounded in *In Search of the Miraculous* (Arkana, 1988), *The Psychology of Man's Possible Evolution* and *The Fourth Way* (Arkana, 1986). These methods are further elucidated in *A Further Record* (Arkana, 1986). He also wrote a novel, *Strange Life of Ivan Osokin* (Arkana, 1987), and two short stories published as *Talks with a Devil* (Arkana, 1988).

P. D. OUSPENSKY

CONSCIENCE

THE SEARCH FOR TRUTH

INTRODUCTION BY
MERRILY E. TAYLOR

ARKANA

LONDON AND NEW YORK

First published in 1979
ARKANA edition 1988
ARKANA PAPERBACKS is an imprint of
Routledge & Kegan Paul Ltd.
11 New Fetter Lane, London EC4P 4EE

Published in the USA by
Routledge
in association with Methuen Inc.
29 West 35th Street, New York, NY 10001

Printed in Great Britain
by Cox and Wyman Ltd.,
Reading

British Library Cataloguing in Publication Data
Ouspensky, P D
Conscience
1. Man
I. Title
128   BD450
ISBN 1–85063–102–6

The compiler of these essays wishes to state that, though formulated
with more precision by Ouspensky, some of these ideas were first
introduced into Europe by G. I. Gurdjieff

B. F. H.

Contents

Introduction *by Merrily E. Taylor*   1

1 · Memory   13

2 · Surface Personality   49

3 · Self-Will   87

4 · Negative Emotions   115

5 · Notes on Work   135

Introduction

In approaching any of the published works of P. D. Ouspensky, from *Tertium Organum* (first released in Russia in 1912, subsequently translated and published in England in 1920, re-issued many times since) to this new collection of short works, it is important to remember that Ouspensky himself put small faith in the written word as the primary method of reaching the Truth. Not that 'O' (as members of his circle called him among themselves) had any contempt for scholarship or the desire for access to knowledge. A voracious but discriminating reader himself, Ouspensky was six years of age when he first read Turgenev — a clear indication of extraordinary talent at so young an age. By the age of twelve he had devoured most of the literature in natural science and psychology available to him. By the time he was sixteen, according to his own testimony, he had decided to take no formal degrees, but to concentrate his studies on those aspects of knowledge which were outside and above the traditional fields of study. 'The professors were killing science', he said, 'in the same way as priests were killing religion'. None of the established sciences went far enough, he felt, in exploring the other dimensions which surely existed; they stopped, as Ouspensky put it, at a 'blank wall'.

Ouspensky's subsequent reluctance to depend upon writing as a means of conveying knowledge was based upon two major points, both integral to the system he taught. First, was the importance of working upon one's own development with, and through, a school or

structured group environment. Ouspensky's philosophy
was based on the idea that man was a machine, moving
through his existence in a dream-like, mechanistic state,
and that in order to tap his full potential he had to awake
through a disciplined attempt to 'self-remember', — to be
able to become fully aware of himself at any time. Self-
remembering was difficult, requiring a series of steps in a
definite order together with the help of a school; the
eventual reward, through self-study, control, and the
transformation of negative emotions, was the attainment
of objective consciousness. This was an awakened state in
which a man, released from his state of 'waking sleep',
would be capable of seeing the higher reality ('esoteric
knowledge') invisible to him in his ordinary, undeveloped
level of being. The key in all this, of course, was school
work based on the principle that development of knowledge
and growth of being must proceed together for right
understanding. Unlike many other systems, Ouspensky's
could not be successful for the individual alone through
contemplation, or be understood solely by the exercise of
the intellectual faculty. It was for this reason that
Ouspensky stressed throughout his life that 'the System
could not be learned from any book'. Although chapters
of his book *In Search of the Miraculous: Fragments of an
Unknown Teaching*[1] were occasionally read aloud to older
members of his London groups, they were used there not
only to spark discussion, but also to show the level and
intensity of work in the original Russian group. All of
Ouspensky's books should consequently be seen as
introductions to the work of the system rather than as
'guidebooks' for the undertaking of that work.

1 New York, Harcourt, Brace, 1949; London, Routledge & Kegan
Paul, 1950.

The second major reason for Ouspensky's qualms about the value of the book as a teaching device was his own considerable respect for the power of the word. As a distinguished journalist in pre-revolutionary Russia, Ouspensky had earned his living with words and was well aware of both their effectiveness and their intractability. Words well put together on a page could convey a thought as ordinary speech could not; on the other hand, a less-than-perfect written sentence could, by its very ambiguity, obscure more than it revealed. So conscious was Ouspensky of the importance of the right word in the right context that he often revised a manuscript again and again, taking years after the first writing. A typical example is his novel *Strange Life of Ivan Osokin,* written in 1905 but not published until 1915. Several of his books, including the well-known *In Search of the Miraculous: Fragments of an Unknown Teaching,* were never approved by him for publication at all. *In Search of the Miraculous* appeared as a manuscript as early as 1925, was read aloud to members of Ouspensky's London groups in the 1930s, went through a number of revisions, and was still unpublished at Ouspensky's death in 1947.

People who knew Ouspensky well and who attended his meetings often recall his emphasis upon the selection of the correct word to define a given state, his refusal to get involved with religious and philosophical jargon, and his realization that no statement is meaningful if taken out of context. One of his former pupils commented that 'if someone began a question with "Mr. Ouspensky said last week . . . " he would hear the question out and then ask, "But in what connection did I say that?" ' They also remember his respect for the rather awesome authority of the published word — that is, the prospect that a philosophy once captured in a book is in danger of becoming entombed there, subject to endless dissection or taken as gospel and becoming as dead as the laws of the Medes and Persians. Hence Ouspensky's realization of the risk in deciding to publish a book, and his caution in making the decision to see his own work between hard covers.

Ouspensky was a master of the spoken as well as of the written word. He was first a teacher, and the five works in this small volume are the product, not of a man writing alone in a study, but of a teacher explaining a system of ideas which could only be slowly appreciated and correctly understood by thoughtful questions from his listeners and their sincere wish to learn. For twenty-six years (1921–47), Ouspensky presided at meetings at which those who were interested in working within the system could hear a basic lecture, then clarify its meaning for themselves by asking precise questions (proper formulation of a question was an important part of the self-discipline required by Ouspensky). As one of the members of O's circle recalls:

> The lectures were read for him to groups of sixty or seventy people once a week over a period of three months. Meetings lasted for two hours; generally half a lecture was read at each meeting and then questions were invited which Ouspensky himself would answer. . . . Shorthand notes were kept of most of Ouspensky's meetings and a long compilation was made of extracts from them after his death and published as *The Fourth Way* in 1957. There is much material for study in this book . . . but the nuggets are hard to extract.

The present volume consists of five short essays which were originally printed as books from 1952 to 1955, after Ouspensky's death and prior to the putting together of *The Fourth Way*. The books were printed for private distribution — in no case were more than 300 copies produced — were not sold, and have been unavailable to the general public until this time.

Like *The Fourth Way*, the five books in this volume were constructed from things said by Ouspensky at his meetings; unlike the scope of that larger volume, each essay here concentrates upon an important tenet of the system, so that the 'nuggets' become easier 'to extract'. The value of this identifying and synthesizing of concepts is that, taken together, the essays cover the practical psychological side of the system communicated by Ouspensky; taken separately, each may be grasped at a single sitting and may thus serve as a 'key' to approaching the wealth of material contained in Ouspensky's longer books. The greatest care was taken in selecting passages from the Ouspensky meeting transcripts, in editing them for continuity, and in avoiding distortion or embroidery of Ouspensky's ideas. In nearly every case, Ouspensky's comments are transcribed 'verbatim'. It should be remembered, of course, that the meetings from whose transcripts these books were produced took place over a period of nearly thirty years, and that during those years Ouspensky enlarged, deepened, and refined his thoughts. In addition, complete understanding of some of the terms employed in these essays depends upon a knowledge of 'special meanings in connection with a system of the Fourth Way which Ouspensky taught'. Those seeking a more cohesive overview of Ouspensky's philosophy or further elaboration upon the meaning of certain terms employed in this book, should proceed from this 'sample' to his longer books, including *A New Model of the Universe; In Search of the Miraculous: Fragments of an Unknown Teaching;* and *The Psychology of Man's Possible Evolution.* (Published after Ouspensky's death, this small book contains the text of the lectures which were read to 'new people' at Ouspensky's meetings during the four-to-six month introductory process. It has been said that a reading of it is 'essential . . . for any serious study of the ideas'. Despite the foregoing caveats, the lay reader need have no hesitation in approaching the five works herein contained, for there is much in them to be understood by anyone who is aware, however vaguely, that there is more to existence than would appear to be revealed by the humdrum patterns of everyday life. One cannot help but respond, for example, to Ouspensky's haunting words in the early pages of *Memory*:

> Man has occasional moments of self-consciousness, but he has no command over them. They come and go by themselves, being controlled by external circumstances and occasional associations or emotions. The question arises: is it possible to acquire command over these fleeting moments of consciousness, to evoke them more often and to keep them longer, or even make them permanent?

Since the Second World War, of course, there has been a steady growth of public interest in the study of 'consciousness', not as it is defined by the medical sciences but as something else — an awareness and perception of a world above and beyond our ordinary experience. In the last twenty years, especially, we have seen the emergence of various techniques seeking to raise the level of consciousness or 'being', from techniques employing drugs to those based wholly or in part on the ancient Eastern religions. In addition, throughout the so-called 'legitimate sciences' there has been renewed and serious study in those areas once labelled part of the Occult: extrasensory perception, psychic phenomena, additional dimensions, bio-feedback, telepathy, and other subjects once considered the province of fortune-tellers and charlatans. It could be said that the entire everyday world is coming around to the observation made four hundred years ago in *Hamlet*: 'There are more things in heaven and earth, Horatio, than are dreamt of in your philosophy.'

It is for these reasons that it is appropriate today to re-issue these five books, at a time when there is a re-awakening of interest in P. D. Ouspensky and in other philosophers, once outside the mainstream, who said long ago that there is 'a knowledge which surpasses all ordinary human knowledge and is inaccessible to ordinary people, but which exists somewhere and belongs to somebody'. Ouspensky's papers, now held in the Collection of Manuscripts and Archives of the Yale University Library (the P. D. Ouspensky Memorial Collection was opened to scholars with a large exhibition in October 1978), show ample evidence of the fact that P. D. O. and his 'people' were seeking a way to reach that higher knowledge long before it was fashionable — or even acceptable — to do so. Nor did following 'the Fourth Way' demand monetary contributions, the taking of drugs, or even a slavish acceptance of the statements made by Ouspensky himself — indeed, one of his circle recalls, 'He asked us not to accept any ideas that could not be proven in practice.' What *was* necessary was the willingness to accept one's own mechanicalness and lack of unifying consciousness, and to summon the will to self-remember in order to overcome the one and acquire the other. The reader who finds himself bewildered by the conflicting objectives and methods of many of today's cults and philosophies should find a welcome clarity in the goals of Ouspensky as expressed in *Surface Personality*: 'The aim of this system is to bring man to conscience.'

The reader will gain the most from these five short

works of Ouspensky by reading them rather than reading *about* them. Nevertheless, a few short explanations:

Memory: Extracts from the Sayings and Writings of
P. D. O. about Memory, Self-Remembering and Recurrence
Like the other works in this volume, *Memory* was privately printed at the Stourton Press in Cape Town, South Africa. Its date is 1953. The first four sections of the book can be found in a slightly different form in *The Psychology of Man's Possible Evolution.* Section five is quoted from *In Search of the Miraculous*; sections six and seven have been reconstructed from records of some of Ouspensky's meetings in London and New York.

The chief theme of *Memory* is that in reality we remember very little of our lives, and that this is because we remember *only* conscious moments. Ouspensky's 'consciousness' was not merely the opposite of sleep, or unconsciousness; it was an awareness of self, a self-remembering. Ouspensky then discusses how we may attain true self-consciousness and with it, full memory and an appreciation of being alive (as opposed to merely existing in a mechanistic state).

Surface Personality: A Study of Imaginary Man
This book, published in 1954, is composed entirely of things said by P. D. O. in meetings from 1930 to 1944. *Surface Personality* is organized around Ouspensky's statement that 'The chief feature of our being is that we are many, not one.' Because man is not fully aware of himself, he is also not aware of the many contradictory desires, beliefs, emotions, and prejudices which sway him from one moment to the next; he has no 'centre of gravity', and, lacking that, is incapable of sustaining a fixed goal for any length of time. Although he may believe he is

determining his own life's direction, a man is actually buffeted from one desire to another by an assortment of outside influences. Man can overcome this state only by becoming aware of his multiple selves and by seeking to develop his true self by stopping the expression of negative emotions, identification, lying, and the other elements of 'false personality'.

Self-Will: A Compilation of things said by P. D. Ouspensky mainly about the need to subjugate Self-Will as a preparation for the growth of Will

Two hundred copies of this book were printed at Cape Town in 1955; the text was printed from answers given to questions at meetings held by P. D. O. in London and New York between 1935 and 1944. Man, says Ouspensky, has no will, only self-will ('wanting to have our own way') and wilfulness ('wanting to do something simply because we shouldn't'). Both grow out of the momentary passing desires of the many 'I's,' or selves, of which man consists. True will is present only in conscious man and is a goal to be obtained through the system; we gain will by exercising in work through the system, in a school situation. Self-will and wilfulness are particularly difficult to obliterate because they are part of our illusion that we are already conscious and able to 'do' — that is, accomplish something by original intent rather than as a mechanistic, reflex response to outside influences.

A Synthesis of Some of the Sayings and Writings of P. D. O. on the subject of Negative Emotions

This work, originally printed in 1953, was taken from the unpublished writings and sayings of P. D. O., with the exception of some definitions of terms which were taken from the privately published *Psychological Lectures,*

1934–40. 'Negative emotions' are all emotions of violence
or depression. Ouspensky stated that such emotions were
useless and destructive, and that despite our protests to the
contrary they arose not from outside provocations but
from within ourselves. However, negative emotions were
artificial — arising out of identification (our incapability
of separating ourselves from the objects, people, or
emotions around us) — and hence could be destroyed once
we became aware of them and attempted to suppress them
through self-remembering. The first step in eliminating
negative emotions is to limit their expression; when this
happens, it will then become possible to get at the root of
negative emotions themselves.

Notes on Work

Notes on Work, first printed in 1952, consists of three
short essays: 'Notes on Decision to Work', 'Notes on Work
on Oneself', and 'What is School?' All deal with the degree
of individual commitment required from one beginning
work in the system. The chief message of *Notes on Work* is
contained in Ouspensky's opening paragraph: 'Think very
seriously before you decide to work on yourself with the
idea of changing yourself . . . this work admits of no
compromise and it requires a great amount of self-discipline
and readiness to obey all rules . . . '

These five works were once printed in very limited
quantities and made available to a small group of people
who had devoted themselves for years to the study of
Ouspensky's philosophy. The decision to reprint *Memory,
Surface Personality, Self-Will, Negative Emotions* and
Notes on Work for presentation to a larger audience is
based on renewed public enthusiasm, much of it taking the

form of inquiries about the P. D. Ouspensky Memorial Collection at the Yale University Library. It is hoped that the many scholars and interested lay people who have come to know Ouspensky through that, and other, avenues will gain further insight into P. D. O. — and themselves — by discovering this remarkable new collection.

Merrily E. Taylor

1

Memory

*

Extracts from the Sayings and
Writings of P. D. Ouspensky about
Memory, Self-Remembering and Recurrence

Foreword

The purpose of this chapter, *Memory,* is to bring together things said and written by Ouspensky about memory, self-remembering and recurrence. The contents of *Memory* are not definitive but are supplementary to what Ouspensky wrote about these subjects in *Tertium Organum* and *A New Model of the Universe. Memory* cannot be understood without reference to those books and without a knowledge of Ouspensky's system of studying the Fourth Way.

The first four sections of this book can be found printed in a slightly different form in *The Psychology of Man's Possible Evolution.* Section five is quoted from *In Search of the Miraculous.* Sections six and seven have been reconstructed from records of some of Ouspensky's meetings in London and New York. These two sections do not always use Ouspensky's exact words because a verbatim record of question and answer would be too diffuse, but great care has been taken not to alter or embroider the meaning of Ouspensky's words in any way.

Summary of Contents

What is meant by 'consciousness' 16.   What we actually remember 16.
Degrees of consciousness 17.   Consciousness and will 18.   The first
obstacle to consciousness 18.   Memory as a set of gramophone
records 19.   Records connected by association 20.   Giving a
direction to our thoughts about consciousness 21.   Self-remembering
22.   Becoming conscious at will 22.   Alchemy 23.   Some
realizations about self-remembering 23.   An attempt at self-
remembering described 25.   Different kinds of memory 27.
Increasing memory 27.   Identification 27.   Remembering the
past 28.   Cross-roads 28.   Use of the theory of recurrence 28.
Recurrence is in eternity 29.   Study of recurrence through children
29.   Unexpected tendencies in children 29.   Heredity 29.   Fully
formed mentality of babies 30.   Memory of a very early dream 31.
Tendencies and recurrence 32.   This work did not exist before 32.
Eternity of the moment beyond the grasp of our minds 33.   Only
man no. 5 can recur as such 33.   Tendency and habit 33.   Problems
of time need mathematical thinking 34.   Memory of recurrence
needs six dimensions 35.   Dimensions explained 35.   Time and
eternity 36.   Necessary to remember oneself in order to have
memory 36.   Accidental self-remembering 37.   Idea of recurrence
useful but not necessary in this sytem 37.   First efforts at self-
remembering 37.   Consciousness of one's function 38.   Use of
cross-roads in relation to recurrence 38.   Possibilities of the
moment 39.   Consciousness and memory 40.   Continuity of
effort 40.   Self-remembering at the Gare du Nord 40.   Knowledge
and being 41.   Permanent centre of gravity 41.   Immortality and
memory 42.   Recurrence and memory 42.   Different kinds of
memory 43.   Spoiling memory 44.   Preparing for recurrence 45.
Triads and recurrence 46.   Recurrence and time 46.   Material for
understanding 46.   Effect of recurrence modified by capacities 47.

1

In most cases in ordinary language, the word consciousness is used as an equivalent to the word intelligence (in the sense of mind activity), or as an alternative for it. In reality, consciousness is a particular kind of 'awareness' in man, awareness of himself, awareness of who he is, what he feels or thinks, or where he is at the moment.

According to the system we are studying, man has the possibility of four states of consciousness. They are: *sleep, waking state, self-consciousness* and *objective consciousness.* But although he has the possibility of these four states of consciousness man actually lives only in two states: one part of his life passes in sleep, and the other part in what is called 'waking state', though in reality it differs very little from sleep.

As regards our ordinary memory, or moments of memory, we actually remember only moments of consciousness although we do not see that this is so.

What memory means in a technical sense, I shall explain later. Now I simply want you to turn your attention to your own observations of your memory. You will notice that you remember things differently: some things you remember quite vividly, some very vaguely, and some you do not remember at all. You only *know* that they happened.

This means, for instance, that if you know that some time ago you went to a definite place to speak to someone, you may remember two or three things connected with your conversation with this person; but you may not remember at all how you went there or how you returned. Now if you are asked if you remember how you went there and how you returned, you will say that you remember distinctly, when, in reality, you only know it and *know* where you went; but you do not *remember* it, with the exception possibly of two or three flashes.

You will be astonished when you realize how little you actually remember. And it happens in this way, because you *remember only the moments when you were conscious.* You will understand better what I mean if you try to turn your mind back as far as you can to early childhood, or in any case to something that happened long ago. You will then realize how little you actually remember and how much there is concerning which you simply *know* or *heard that it happened.*

So in reference to the third state of consciousness we can say that man has occasional moments of self-consciousness, but he has no command over them. They come and go by themselves, being controlled by external circumstances and occasional associations or emotions.

The question arises: Is it possible to acquire command over these fleeting moments of consciousness, to evoke them more often and to keep them longer, or even make them permanent?

2

The first or the lowest state of consciousness is sleep. ... Man is surrounded by dreams ... Purely subjective pictures — either reflections of former experiences or reflections of vague perceptions of the moment, such as sounds reaching the sleeping man, sensations coming from the body, slight pains, sensations of tension — fly through the mind, leaving only a very slight trace on the memory and often leaving no trace at all.

The second degree of consciousness comes when man awakes. This second state — the state in which we are now;

the state in which we work, talk, imagine ourselves conscious beings and so forth — we ordinarily call 'waking consciousness' or 'clear consciousness', but really it should be called 'waking sleep' or 'relative consciousness'.

In the state of sleep we can have glimpses of relative consciousness. In the state of relative consciousness we can have glimpses of self-consciousness. But if we want to have more prolonged periods of self-consciousness and not merely glimpses, we must understand that they cannot come by themselves. They need *will action.* This means that frequency and duration of moments of self-consciousness depend on the command one has over oneself. So it means too that consciousness and will are almost one and the same thing, or in any case, aspects of the same thing.

At this point it must be understood that the first obstacle in the way of the development of self-consciousness in man is his conviction that he already possesses self-consciousness, or at any rate that he can have it at any time he likes. It is very difficult to persuade a man that he is not conscious, and cannot be conscious, *at will.* It is particularly difficult because here nature plays a very funny trick. If you ask a man if he is conscious, or if you say to him that he is not conscious, he will answer that he is conscious and that it is absurd to say that he is not, because he hears and understands you. And he will be quite right, although at the same time quite wrong. This is nature's trick. He will be quite right because your question or your remark has made him vaguely conscious for a moment. Next moment consciousness will disappear. But he will remember what you said and what he answered, and he will certainly consider himself conscious.

In reality, acquiring self-consciousness means long and hard work. How can a man agree to this work if he thinks he already possesses the very thing which is promised him as the result of long and hard work? Naturally a man will not begin this work and will not consider it necessary until he becomes convinced that he possesses neither self-consciousness nor all that is connected with it, that is to say, unity or individuality, permanent 'I' and will.

3

[In order to understand the following paragraphs it must be realized that the common view that man has only one mind (the intellectual mind) is mistaken. In reality, the nervous system is divided according to the functions of the body, and each division has its own mind. Ouspensky's use of the word 'centre' differs from the current scientific meaning because it includes both the particular mind in control and also the nerves and subsidiary collections of nerve cells which connect it with other parts of the body.]

We must find the reason why we cannot develop more quickly without a long period of school-work. We know that when we learn something we accumulate new material in our memory. But what is our memory? And what is new material?

To understand this we must learn to regard each centre as a separate and independent machine, consisting of a sensitive matter which, by its function, is similar to the matter from which gramophone records are made. All that happens to us, all that we see, all that we hear, all that we feel, all that we learn, is registered on these records. This means that all external and internal events leave certain impressions on the records. 'Impressions' is a very good word because they actually are impressions or imprints that are left. An impression can be deep, or it can be slight, or it can be simply a glancing impression that disappears very quickly and leaves no trace behind it. But whether deep or slight it is an impression. And these impressions on records are all that we have, all our possessions. Everything that we know, everything that we have learned, everthing that we have experienced, is all there on our records.

Exactly in the same way our thought-processes, calculations and speculations consist only of comparing our records with each other, listening to them again and again, trying to understand them by putting them together, and so on. We can think of nothing new, nothing that is not on our records. We can neither say nor do anything that does not correspond to something on the records. We cannot invent a new thought, just as we cannot invent a new animal, because all our ideas of animals are created from our observation of existing animals.

The impressions on our records are connected by associations. Associations connect impressions received simultaneously or in some way similar to one another.

Since memory depends on consciousness and we actually remember only the moments when we had flashes of consciousness, it is quite clear that different simultaneous impressions connected together will remain longer in the memory than unconnected impressions. In the flash of self-consciousness, or even near to it, all the impressions of the moment are connected and remain connected in the memory. The same applies to impressions connected by their inner similarity. If we are more conscious at the moment of receiving an impression, we connect the new impression more definitely with similar old impressions and they remain connected in the memory. On the other hand, if we receive impressions in a state of sleep, we simply do not notice them and their traces disappear before they can be appreciated or associated.

[At one of his meetings Ouspensky was asked whether all the imprints on our records are formed in this life or whether we are born with some of them. He answered:]

The imprints in instinctive centre are born with us; they are already there, so are a very few things in the emotional centre. The rest come in this life; in moving and intellectual centres everything has to be learnt.

4

In order to understand more clearly what I am going to say, you must try to remember that we have no control over our consciousness. When I said that we can become more conscious, or that a man can be made conscious for a moment simply by asking him if he is conscious or not, I used the words 'conscious' and 'consciousness' in a relative sense. There are so many degrees of consciousness and every higher degree means more 'conscious' in relation to a lower degree. But although we have no control over consciousness itself, we have a certain control over our thinking about consciousness, and we can construct our thinking in such a way as to bring consciousness. What I mean is that by giving to our thoughts a direction which they would have in a moment of consciousness, we can, in this way, induce consciousness.

Now try to formulate what you noticed when you tried to observe yourself. You should have noticed three things. First, that you do not *remember yourself*, that is to say, you are not aware of yourself at the time when you try to observe yourself. Secondly, that observation is made difficult by the incessant stream of thoughts, images, echoes of conversation, fragments of emotions flowing through your mind and very often distracting your attention from observation. And thirdly, that as soon as you start self-observation something in you starts imagination, and self-observation — if you really tried it — is a constant struggle with imagination.

Now this is the chief point in work upon oneself. If one realizes that all the difficulties in the work depend on the fact that one cannot remember oneself, one already knows what one must do. One *must try* to remember oneself.

In order to do this one must struggle with mechanical thoughts and one must struggle with imagination. If one does this conscientiously and persistently one will see results in a comparatively short time. But one must not think that it is easy or that one can master this practice immediately. *Self-remembering,* as it is called, is a very difficult thing to learn to practise. It must not be based on expectation of results, otherwise one becomes lost in thinking about one's own efforts. It must be based on the realization of the fact that we do not remember ourselves, and that at the same time we *can* remember ourselves if we try sufficiently hard and in the right way.

We cannot become conscious at will, at the moment when we want to, because we have no command over states of consciousness. But we can remember ourselves for a short time at will because we have a certain command over our thoughts. And if we start remembering ourselves by the special construction of our thoughts, that is, by the realization that we do not remember ourselves; that no one remembers himself, and by realizing what this means, this realization will bring us to consciousness.

You must understand that we have found the weak spot in the wall of our mechanicalness. This is the knowledge that we do not remember ourselves and the realization that we can try to remember ourselves. With the understanding of the necessity for actual change in ourselves, the possibility of work begins.

Later on you will learn that the practice of self-remembering, connected with self-observation and with the struggle against imagination, has not only a psychological meaning, but it also changes the sublest part of our metabolism and produces definite chemical, or perhaps it is better to say alchemical, effects in our body. So from psychology we come to alchemy; to the idea of the transformation of coarse elements into finer ones.

5

[Self-remembering and its effect upon memory are described in a more personal way than in the previous section in *Fragments of an Unknown Teaching*,[1] from which the following paragraphs are quoted.]

... all that my attempts at self-remembering had shown me, very soon convinced me that I was faced with an *entirely new problem which science and philosophy had not, so far, come across* ...

I saw that the problem consisted in directing attention on oneself without weakening or obliterating the attention directed on something else. Moreover this 'something else' could as well be within me as outside me.

The very first attempts ... showed me its possibility. At the same time I saw two things clearly.

In the first place I saw that self-remembering resulting from this method had nothing in common with 'self-

1.P. D. Ouspensky, *In Search of the Miraculous*, (New York, 1949), pp. 118–21.

feeling', or 'self-analysis'. It was a new and very interesting state with a strangely familiar flavour.

And secondly I realized that moments of self-remembering do occur in life, although rarely. Only the deliberate production of these moments created the sensation of novelty. Actually I had been familiar with them from early childhood. They came either in new and unexpected surroundings, in a new place, among new people while travelling, for instance, when suddenly one looks about one and says: *How strange! I and in this place;* or in very emotional moments, in moments of danger, in moments when it is necessary to keep one's head, when one hears one's own voice and sees and observes oneself from the outside.

I saw quite clearly that my first recollections of life, in my own case very early ones, were moments of *self-remembering.* This last realization revealed much else to me. That is, I saw that I really only remember those moments of the past in which *I remembered myself.* Of the others *I know only that they took place.* I am not able wholly to revive them, to experience them again. But the moments when I had remembered myself were alive and were in no way different from the present. I was still afraid to come to conclusions. But I already saw that I stood upon the threshold of a very great discovery. I had always been astonished at the weakness and the insufficiency of our memory. So many things disappear. For some reason or other the chief absurdity of life for me consisted in this. Why experience so much in order to forget it afterwards? Besides there was something degrading in this. A man feels something which seems to him very big, he thinks he will never forget it; one or two years pass by — and nothing remains of it. It now became clear to me why this was so and why it could not be otherwise. If our memory really

keeps alive only moments of self-remembering, it is clear
why our memory is so poor . . .

Sometimes self-remembering was not successful; at
other times it was accompanied by curious observations.

I was once walking along the Liteiny towards the
Nevsky, and in spite of all my efforts I was unable to keep
my attention on self-remembering. The noise, movement,
everything distracted me. Every minute I lost the thread
of attention, found it again, and then lost it again. At last
I felt a kind of ridiculous irritation with myself and I
turned into the street on the left having firmly decided to
keep my attention on the fact that *I would remember
myself* at least for some time, at any rate until I reached
the following street. I reached the Nadejdinskaya without
losing the thread of attention except, perhaps, for short
moments. Then I again turned towards the Nevsky
realizing that, in quiet streets, it was easier for me not to
lose the line of thought and wishing therefore to test
myself in more noisy streets. I reached the Nevsky still
remembering myself, and was already beginning to
experience the strange emotional state of inner peace and
confidence which comes after great efforts of this kind.
Just round the corner on the Nevsky was a tobacconist's
shop where they made my cigarettes. Still remembering
myself I thought I would call there and order some
cigarettes.

Two hours later I *woke up* in the Tavricheskaya, that is,
far away. I was going by *izvostchik* to the printers. The
sensation of awakening was extraordinarily vivid. I can
almost say that I *came to*. I remembered everything at
once. How I had been walking along the Nadejdinskaya,
how I had been remembering myself, how I had thought
about cigarettes, and how at this thought I seemed all at
once to fall and disappear into a deep sleep.

At the same time, while immersed in this sleep, I had continued to perform consistent and expedient actions. I left the tobacconist, called at my flat in the Liteiny, telephoned to the printers. I wrote two letters. Then again I went out of the house. I walked on the left side of the Nevsky up to the Gostinoy Dvor intending to go to the Offitzerskaya. Then I had changed my mind as it was getting late. I had taken an *izvostchik* and was driving to the Kavalergardskaya to my printers. And on the way while driving along the Tavricheskaya I began to feel a strange uneasiness, as though I had forgotten something. — *And suddenly I remembered that I had forgotten to remember myself.*

6

[At his meetings in London between 1935 and 1941 and at meetings in New York in 1944 and 1945, Ouspensky was asked many questions about memory and recurrence. The section which follows consists of a reconstruction of answers at his London meetings to some of these questions. Section 7 attempts to reconstruct some of the answers given in New York, in a similar way. For the sake of continuity and to avoid repetition, some of the questions are either presumed or have been incorporated in Ouspensky's answers. Otherwise they appear within quotation marks, to distinguish them from Ouspensky's words which — as they form the bulk of the text — are not set within quotation marks. The order of the questions has been rearranged and only those which are connected with memory and recurrence have been included.]

Memory is a strange thing. Everyone has his own combination of capacities for memory. One person remembers some things more; another remembers other things better. You cannot say that one is better than the other. Memory may disappear; there are many different degrees of it. Something may be forgotten and then brought up again by special methods, or it may disappear altogether.

'Why do some people have a greater facility for playing ball games than others?'

There are many different kinds of moving centre with different kinds of memory. There is not a single man similar to another man. One can do one thing better; another, another thing. There are thousands of impressions so that the combinations are always different. I have spoken several times about the different kinds of man — no. 1, no. 2, no. 3 and so on. One remembers one kind of impression better; another, another kind.

'Does a life consist of memories from one moment to another?'

No that is too complicated. You know that there are many different sorts of memory. And memory is passive; you do not use it. Life can be said to be a process.

'What can one do to increase one's memory?'

If you remember yourself more, your memory will be better.

'Until I came into the system I had a very clear memory of something which happened some time ago. Now, if I recall it, it is just a memory of a memory. Is this due to being a little more awake?'

It was probably connected with strong identification. When you look at it without identification it becomes fainter and may disappear.

'Is complete non-identification self-consciousness?'

Identification and self-consciousness are two different sides of the same thing.

'Is it of practical use to think of the events of one's past life when trying to self-remember? I mean, with a view to fixing them for any future recurrence.'

No, this is not practical. First it is necessary for you to be sure that future recurrence exists. Secondly, it is necessary for you to be sure of remembering yourself. If you put it to yourself as you did in your question, it will turn into imagination, nothing else. But if you try first of all to remember yourself without adding anything to it, and then — when you can — also to remember about your past life, and try to find cross-roads; then, in combination, they will be very useful. Only do not think that you can do it; you cannot do it yet.

'What are cross-roads?'

Cross-roads are moments when one can 'do'. A moment comes when one can help in this work or not. If an opportunity comes and one misses it, another may not come for a year or even longer. There are periods in ordinary conditions when nothing happens, and then there come cross-roads. All life consists of streets and cross-roads.

Recurrence can be useful if one begins to remember and if one begins to change and not go by the same circle each time, but do what one wants and what one thinks better. But if one does not know about recurrence, or even if one knows and does not do anything, then there is no advantage in it at all. Then, it is generally the same things repeated and repeated.

'Am I right in supposing that it is man's essence which recurs?'

Quite right. We know very little about recurrence. Some day we may try to collect what can be taken as reliable in all that is said about recurrence, and see how we can think about it. But it is only theory.

Recurrence is in eternity; it is not the same life. This life ends and time ends. There is a theory, and this system admits the theory, that time can be prolonged. I have no evidence. Think how many attempts to find out about time have been made by spiritualists and others. But there is no evidence.

The easiest way of studying recurrence is by studying children. If we had enough material we could answer many questions. Why, for instance, do strange tendencies appear in children, quite opposed to their surrounding circumstances and quite new to the people who surround them? That happens sometimes, in many different ways. And they may be very strong tendencies that change life and go in quite unexpected directions, when there is nothing in heredity to account for them.

As I have often said, the idea of heredity in man does not work. It is a fantastic idea. It works in dogs and horses but not in man.

'Does the question of types come into that?'

Yes, but we know nothing about types. At least not enough to speak about them. This is why in most cases it happens that parents do not understand their children and the children do not understand their parents. They never could really understand one another sufficiently or rightly, because they are quite different people, strangers to one another, who have just happened to meet accidentally at a certain station and then go in different directions again.

The study of recurrence must begin with the study of children's minds; particularly before they begin to speak. If children could remember this time they would remember very interesting things. But, unfortunately, when they begin to speak they become real children and they forget after six months or a year. It is very seldom that people remember what they thought before that, at a very early age. If they could do so they would remember themselves such as they were when grown up. They were not children at all; then, later they became children. If they could remember their early mentality it would be the same mentality as grown-up people have. That is what is interesting.

'Do you know why a child should remember its grown-up mind and not its previous child's mind?'

We have so little material by which to judge. I speak only of the way in which it can be studied. Suppose we were to try to remember what our minds were like at a very early age, trying not to let imagination come in. Suppose we were to find they were of one sort or another. Anything we found would be material. In literature you find very little because people do not understand how to study recurrence, but, within my own experience, I have met with very interesting things. Some people I knew had recollections of the first years of their lives, and they all had the same impression which was that their mentality was not a child's mentality. How they took people, how they recognized people; it was not a child's psychology. They had fully formed minds with quite grown-up reactions such as you cannot imagine could have been formed in six months of unconscious life. Such minds must have existed before if their recollections were really correct. But, as I say, it is very difficult to find material, and most people do not remember at all.

'Why should that early memory disappear when the child learns to talk?'

The child begins to imitate other children and do exactly what grown-up people expect from him. They expect him to be a stupid child and he becomes a stupid child.

'How is it possible to know what a baby remembers? I

thought that one was born with one's centres completely blank, and that one remembered with centres.'

This is a strange thing. Yet the people I spoke of — who do not differ much from other people — have quite definite recollections of their first months even, and they think that they saw people as grown-up people do — not as children would. They do not try to reconstruct elaborate pictures from scattered and fragmentary recollections; they have quite definite impressions of houses, people and so on. They seem to have had a quite grown-up mentality.

'I can remember things when I was two years old which did not happen at all. How can one verify what a baby remembered before it could speak?'

How do you know that they did not happen? It could have been a dream. I had an experience of that kind. I remember that when I was quite a child I was in some place near Moscow and the picture of the place remained in my memory. Actually, I was not there until about four years after that. Then, when I went there, I saw that the place was not the same as it had been in my memory, and I realized that my memory had been a dream.

About the question of former lives: I think some people can remember something, although only in very rare cases, since to remember implies already a certain definite degree of development. Ordinary man — no. 1, no. 2 and no. 3 — has no apparatus for such memory. Essence is mechanical. It does not live by itself; it has no special thinking apparatus, but has to think through personality, and personality has no experience.

'When you said, "Observe children", what did you mean?'

That is what is so difficult. If you observe tendencies on a big scale you can find quite unexpected tendencies. You cannot say that they are the result of a certain reason or of surroundings, because quite unexpected tendencies can appear and disappear. They will continue throughout life afterwards. In such a case, according to the theory of recurrence, the tendency may have been acquired in a previous life in much later years, and then it appears very early in this life.

'From the point of view of recurrence then, may it not be that some important actions that we make between now and the time that we die are really responsible for our tendencies now?'

You mean in previous lives. Quite possibly. Only, remember one thing, this work did not exist before. It may be that other work did, (there are many kinds,) but not this. It did not exist before, I am perfectly sure of that.

'What I mean is that it seems such a huge idea to think that between now and the time when we die, we may make fatal actions which will give us tendencies for the next time.'

Certainly, in every moment of our lives we may create tendencies that we may not be able to get rid of for ten lives. That is why this point is always emphasized in Indian literature. It may be in fairy-tale form but the principle is the same.

'Is it possible to learn something of essence through memories of childhood?'

You can if you have a good memory and can find things in yourself that have changed and things that do not change.

'Is there any sign by which you can tell that we have not been in this house before?'

No one can tell. I only know that I have not been in this house before.

'Then we have not either'.

I do not know. But you will be much nearer to the truth

if you begin with *this* as the first time. If we did something before, then it was only so much as made this possible.

'Does the idea of parallel time mean that all moments continually exist?'

Yes, it is very difficult to think about it. Certainly it means eternity of the moment, but our minds cannot think in that way. Our mind is a very limited machine. We must think in the easiest way and make allowance for it. It is easier to think of repetition than of the eternal existence of the moment. You must understand that our mind cannot formulate rightly things as they are. We can only make approximate formulations which are nearer to truth than our ordinary thinking. That is all that is possible. Our mind and our language are very rough instruments and we have to deal with very fine matters and fine problems.

'Having met the system in one recurrence, will one meet it again in the next?'

It depends upon what one did with the system. One could meet the system and say, 'What nonsense these people talk'. So it depends upon how much effort one made. If one made efforts one could have acquired something, and that might remain if it was not only in *Surface Personality*; if it was not only formatory.

'If one dies as man no. 4 does one recur as man no. 4 or could one lose it by imitating negative emotions and so on?'

No, only man no. 5 can recur as man no. 5. He may not know it, but things will be easier for him. No. 4 has to make again only it will be easier and earlier.

'Could a tendency in one recurrence become habit in the next?'

It depends on the tendency. If it is mechanical it will become a habit; if it is a conscious tendency it cannot become a habit because they are two different things.

All acquired tendencies repeat themselves. One person acquires a tendency to study or to be interested in certain things. He will be interested again. Another acquires a tendency to run away from certain things. He will run away again. These tendencies may grow stronger or they may grow in a different direction. There is no guarantee until one reaches some kind of conscious action when one has a certain possibility of trusting oneself.

'Will you explain how it is possible for a man to live co-existent lives simultaneously in two time places at the same time?'

There are many things that look impossible but that is because our thinking apparatus is not good enough to think about such things. It simplifies things too much. These problems need mathematical thinking. For instance, we cannot think about time as a curve but only as a straight line. If we could think of time as a curve, and understand all that that implied, this question of yours would not arise. In this case we are in exactly the same position as plane-beings trying to think of a three-dimensional world. Really there is no problem of this kind. The problem is the structure of our own mind. The aim of all our work is to reach the third and fourth states of consciousness, which means to think through higher centres. If we could do this, then problems of the future life, absurdities like this time question, and so on, would not arise. As things are, we can only make theories. We know more or less how to approach these problems, but we can know nothing definite.

'Can a man be no. 5 in one life and no. 3 in another simultaneously?'

I really do not know. One cannot become no. 5 at once; one has to approach slowly, and if a man develops into no. 5 outside school, then it is a very slow process, so I do not think the difference would be so big from one life to another. I can say only one thing about it. I think that if one knows consciously and fully about recurrence, and can speak about it and accept it, then one cannot fully forget it next time. So if you accept it and know it in one life there is a great chance of remembering much more next time. We have no experience, but you will notice how in literature, history and philosophy people return again and again to this idea of recurrence. They never fully forget it, but it is very difficult to fit it into a three-dimensional world. It needs a five-dimensional world, and the question of remembering really refers already to six dimensions. In the fifth dimension man returns and returns without knowing. Remembering means a certain growth in the sixth dimension.

Dimensions can be understood simply in this way. The fourth dimension is the realization of one possibility of each moment; what we call time. The fifth dimension is repetition of this. The sixth dimension is the realization of *different* possibilities. But it is difficult to think about this so long as we think about time as a straight line. The problem is not a real thing; it is just our weakness, nothing more.

'I do not understand what you mean when you say the fourth dimension is the realization of one possibility.'

Life is the fourth dimension, a circle, the realization of one possibility. When this comes to an end it meets its own beginning. The moment of death corresponds to the moment of birth, and then life begins again, maybe with slight deviations, but they do not mean anything. It always returns to the same line. Breaking a chief tendency, starting this life in a quite different way will be the sixth dimension.

We cannot think of simultaneous moments, we have to

think of one moment following another, though actually they are simultaneous on another scale. For instance, our own experience in relation to small particles such as electrons is that their *eternity* is in our *time*. So why can our *repetition* not be in earth's *time*?

'From what I understand about memory, I do not see how it is possible to remember a previous recurrence. I thought that memory was dependent on the contents of centres which are in personality. How can personality remember recurrence?'

You cannot remember if you do not remember yourself here, in this recurrence. We have lived before. Many facts prove it. The reason why we do not remember is because we did not remember ourselves. The same is true in this life. We do not really remember the things that we do mechanically, we only know that they happened. Only with self-remembering can we remember details.

Personality is always mixed with essence. Memory is in essence, not in personality, but personality can present it quite rightly if memory is sufficiently strong.

'It is very difficult to think about preparing for meeting the system earlier.'

You can prepare nothing. Only remember yourself, then you will remember things better. The whole thing lies in negative emotions: we enjoy them so much that we have no interest in anything else. If you remember yourself now, then you may remember next time.

'Is this the reason for the "I have been here before" feeling? The feeling that one has already some piece of knowledge that one could not possibly have heard?'

I want facts. It may simply be a compound picture of different ideas. If you can really remember something of the kind it means you can self-remember. If you cannot self-remember, it is imagination.

'Is accidental self-remembering of any use for this purpose?'

Accidental self-remembering is a flash for a second. One cannot rely on it.

The only possibility of change begins from the possibility of beginning to remember yourself now. In the system recurrence is not necessary. It may be interesting or useful; you can even start with it, but for actual work on yourself the idea of recurrence is not necessary. That is why we have not heard it from this sytem; it came from outside, from literature and from me. Then you see it fits; it does not contradict. But it is not necessary, because all that we can do, we can do only in this life. If we do not do anything in this life then the next life will be just the same, or it may be the same with slight variations but no positive change.

'Can you explain why attempts at self-remembering seem to be tiring, when tried over some time?'

They ought not to be. A possible explanation is that by making mental effort you unconsciously make physical effort. I think efforts to self-remember can only be tiring if there is something wrong attached. At first we are unable to remember for long at a time and it is better to remind yourself or find methods to remind you about it as often as possible. It may be tiring if you just try to keep your mind on it. That is not really self-remembering, but remembering about self-remembering. This is useful also when you begin to study, but later you must find other methods.

'Any efforts to self-remember that I have made never seemed to get any deeper or on to a higher level. It seems always to be an effort to do it.'

That is the thing. You must do what you can do. First try to remember yourself in the ordinary way, then in difficult moments, the moments in which you forget yourself most easily. After many repetitions of that you will see that it will suddenly pass to a higher level. But that will be without your own direct effort.

'As a man attains a higher state of consciousness, such as self-consciousness, does the speed of his functions change? In other words, can he ever hope that an impression for him will be longer than one ten-thousandth of a second, a breath longer than three seconds, and so on?'

It is possible for the speed of functions to change. This is not similar to the length of impressions and it is useless to examine the dissimilarity. Impressions are longer now. When we speak of a ten-thousandth part of a second we refer only to an impression of the intellectual centre. There are others.

'If a cell could become conscious of its function as part of a man, would it forget that it was a cell? Similarly, if a man became conscious of the way that he contributed to the life of a star, for instance, would he lose the memory of his life as a man, and disappear from the cycle of endlessly recurring lifetimes?'

Quite the opposite process. A cell would remember that it was a cell. The same for man — he would remember that he was a man. It would be the same as self-remembering. He would not lose memory, he would get memory.

'Thinking back over one's life one sees certain cross-ways where some decision was taken which one thinks was bad. Is there any particular thing one can do in this recurrence so that there is less likelihood that we shall make the same mistake in the next?'

Yes, certainly. One can think one can change now in these particular points, and then — if the thinking is sufficently deep — one *will* remember; if it is not so deep one *may* remember. In any case, there is a chance that in time one will manage *not to do* something which one *did* before. Many ideas and things like that can pass through one life to another. For instance, someone asked what one could get from the idea of recurrence. If one became intellectually aware of this idea, and if the idea became part of one's essence — part of one's general attitude towards life — then one could not forget it, and it would be an advantage to know of it early in the next life.

'Are there very definite possibilities for one man at any given moment?'

People think that there are many possibilities. At any rate it looks like that, but really there is only one possibility or sometimes two. Man can only change in the sense of the sixth dimension. Things happen in a certain way and one possibility out of many supposed possibilities is realized at each moment and that makes the line of the fourth dimension. But conscious change, for a definite purpose, which is the idea of work, the idea of development, when you seriously start in this system: that is already a start on the sixth dimension.

'You say there may be two possibilities at a given moment. Do you mean one mechanical and one not?'

No, there may be several mechanical possibilities because small deviations are possible, but you always come back to the line.

7

'What are some of the forms which the first conscious effort takes?'

Being aware of yourself. The realization of 'I am here'. But not words. Feeling. The realization of who you are and where you are.

I advise you to think chiefly about consciousness. How to approach, how to start to understand what consciousness is. We can find examples of consciousness in our own past lives. A moment of consciousness produces very strong memory, so that if we can find moments of clear and very vivid memory in the past, we can know that this is the result of being conscious. With a flash of consciousness you have very clear memories; place, time of day, day of the week and so on. These moments of consciousness give very bright memory.

'In a moment of self-remembering would it be possible to hear something you do not ordinarily hear?'

Quite possible, but it depends what. You cannot expect to hear angels singing.

The only way to increase one's memory is by being more conscious. In no other system is there a method for improving memory. In this system it is definite: *Remember yourself.*

Perhaps in the morning you say you will remember yourself at twelve o'clock. Then you forget all about it but perhaps you remember at one o'clock. That is how things happen. But if you continue this may produce very unexpected results. The whole thing is to create continuity. Glimpses may *happen* but continuity needs effort. At the same time you must not be easily dejected, because the result of work grows slowly. Sometimes, as an exercise in this system, people decide to remember themselves tomorrow at a certain time in certain circumstances. Before the war when people went to Paris I told them to remember themselves at the Gare du Nord. Nobody could. Once a friend was to meet me at the Gare du Nord and I asked him to remember himself when he got there. But he only came with a very worried face saying, 'I have forgotten something you asked me to do, was it something I had to buy?'

It is necessary to distinguish what is self-remembering from what is not. For instance, it is quite different to remember that you said you were going to remember yourself at twelve o'clock, from actually remembering yourself. It is necessary to learn to think. We have much material for right thinking but it is necessary not to forget about it.

In order to become stronger in this system you must accumulate knowledge and being. As being is connected with memory of what we promised ourselves, we can strengthen our being in this way. Memory of our failures can also be very useful but sometimes it is quite useless. If you remember your failures and sit crying or accuse somebody else it will not help.

'Receiving impressions is a mechanical process, is it not?'

They are used in different ways. Take knowledge — one may learn Chinese with enough Chinese words. If one collects enough musical impressions one learns music. Moving energy collects memories of a road or place.

'Did you say that magnetic centre is a group of permanent interests? Would you explain?'

Yes. If we could remember what we liked last week, last month, last year — if we could remember — that would make a permanent centre of gravity. Generally, we forget. But if we can remember and continue to like the same things, that will make a centre of gravity. It is better to remember even what you dislike than not to remember.

'How can memory survive death?'

Death is nothing, you may not notice it. If you do not

notice that you die, you may not notice that you are born.

'Is immortality impossible for man no. 1, 2 and 3?'

Yes, he has to become no. 5. That is one answer. But there may be other answers. For instance, from the point of view of recurrence men 1, 2 and 3 may live again, may turn again, but they do not remember. In order to remember they must become man no. 5.

'What is it that becomes immortal, essence or physical body and soul?'

Only memory. Body is born again; essence is born again; personality is created again. So it is not a question of immortality but of memory. We may live ten thousand times without any advantage if we do not remember. If mechanical immortality were possible it would be of no advantage. We must remember ourselves and remember events; the more the better. Again I remind you: What is useful and necessary to remember is that we do *not* remember; *never* remember and that we do not know that we do not remember.

'Did I understand you to say that if anything of us survived it was memory?'

Probably not quite; because memory usually disappears first, if anything survives. Memory is very unstable.

'It seems to me that in order to realize where we have missed an opportunity in a past life, we should first have to reach a moment of awakening in this life.'

Very good. Only, do that first.

'When I look back at the opportunities missed in this life, I have the feeling that only by being a different kind of person could I have acted differently. From this it seems to me that the only way to affect recurrence is to change one's essence.'

Again, very useful. But how can you do it?

'Would memory of a previous recurrence make it

possible to change one's actions?'

That I do not know. That you will see when you have it.

'A recurring life is not lived exactly as before, is it?'

The beginning is always the same.

'In recurrence through one life to another do we retain the same level of being?'

There are different theories about it. One theory is that if one acquires something in one life it is bound to grow. But there are many other theories.

'Is memory in essence?'

It is better to say that it is connected with 'I's which are in personality. There are many different kinds of memory; ordinary memory, memory of what we hear, memory of this system, memory of smell, memory of roads. But we speak of the memory that we know. It is very easy to spoil this memory.

'There are people with photographic memory. Are they more conscious?'

There are many different kinds of memory. You have a certain kind of memory. Another man has another kind. But you can use your own kind of memory better or worse by being more conscious or less conscious. Memory is in all centres. It may be a little better in one centre than in another but there is only one method of making memory strong — by becoming more conscious. Not only does each centre have its own memory but some kinds of memory belong to essence and some to personality.

'Is memory a function of the body? Can it be compared to movement?'

You can call it a function of the body if you like. But why compare it with movement? One thing is not like another. Memory is something in us, maybe in essence, maybe in personality. We recollect in personality, but memory of taste or smell is in essence. But actually one remembers in personality.

'What must we do to avoid spoiling our memory?'

Work on imagination first; lying second. These two things destroy our memory. When we first spoke of lying people took it as funny; they did not realize that one can destroy one's memory completely. Struggle with imagination also, not just for sport or exercise.

'What can help us to recognize lying in ourselves?'

There are many different things; first, analysis of facts, words and theories. Recognition of other people's lying is very useful and then one bright morning one can come to oneself.

'Does false personality destroy memory?'

Yes, one can say that false personality either destroys or distorts memory.

'Is false personality a form of lying?'

Leave false personality. It is not a form of lying; it is a defence. Avoiding unpleasant results by false personality, one can feel oneself in a certain way.

'Does this spoiling of memory result in physiological change?'

Oh, yes! It may bring complete lunacy. Old psychologists knew about that. They spoke about hysterics and so on. But they did not realize that just by our ordinary psychological play we can spoil memory. Lying about ideas, imagining about ideas and so on.

'What effect would hard work on stopping thoughts have on recurrence?'

Right or wrong, there is promise behind it.

'What is the way towards developing memory in recurrence?'

This is very interesting and very important. It is necessary to develop memory, as it is also possible to destroy memory. According to the theory of recurrence, self-remembering is the only way of developing memory. If one remembers oneself in this life, one will remember next time.

'Is it possible to have emotional feeling in the idea of recurrence?'

Yes, it is possible, particularly if one has even some small recollection. I do not mean everything, but even a slight memory can give interesting emotional understanding.

'When one has a strong feeling of an event having happened before, can one use that to develop memory?'

Oh, it can happen in many different ways; only after a very long and very serious investigation can one come to the conclusion that there may be facts.

'I was wondering whether, if we could do something about this work before we die, it might not help in our next recurrence.'

Yes, what happens before may determine what happens afterwards in many different ways. This is not recurrence.

The question is how can one prepare oneself for recurrence. Suppose in a certain life you want to do something and you find you cannot do it. This needs help. If you cannot physically get this help, you begin to think about it and you realize that you have to prepare for this help during the life before. This life is too late; the next life is too late; the life before is the only chance. Think about it. Perhaps you missed some opportunity. If a man finds that he cannot do something he thinks of a previous time when perhaps he could have done it, or perhaps he could not. Think what this implies.

'Would he not have had to have some memory to realize mistakes in his past life or his lack of preparation?'

There may have been no mistakes, simply lack of preparation. Quite right. One needs preparation. One says one is not prepared. Perhaps one could have been prepared before. Can you do anything about it? It is difficult, I know. But one may realize one is not prepared for a certain thing.

We spoke of six triads. In one triad you can do one thing, in another another thing. But this changes all ideas of recurrence. What could be right for one man would not be right for another. For instance, I said that even theoretical knowledge of recurrence changes one's whole relation to recurrence. It depends, too, how deeply a man knows; there are many degrees.

'Can the Law of Seven be observed in the way things happen or appear?'

The Law of Seven you can speak about when you find two intervals in an octave.

'Can one only see it in operation over a period of many years, or at once?'

You can use memory. That does not mean that you observe actual facts. And you must see two intervals in an octave.

'What can one do to understand the illusion of time?'

One can understand that there is no such thing as time. And why? Because there are facts which show the non-existence of time. Eternal recurrence is not compatible with our present time-sense. The whole thing is in that, so you have to get rid of time-sense. Recurrence refers to eternity, not time.

'Can we keep the pattern from repeating?'

If you have good memory you can.

'You say that if one really accepted the theory of recurrence it would make a difference?'

If one studies, if one works, there is material for understanding. We use understanding and lack of under-standing. If we think enough, we may understand something and we may actually change recurrence.

'Would it be right to say that the only claim for recurrence is that in this life some people remember that they lived before?'

No, that is very weak. Very few people remember and you can always say that they are lying.

'Would not belief in recurrence result in a great urgency to make effort?'

Belief will not help; belief is deadening; it has not sufficient power. But realization may.

We can understand some things by thinking. For example, the question as to whether all people are affected in the same way by recurrence. It is impossible to say simply yes or no because what can be applied to one man cannot be applied to another. For one man it will be the same way, the same house, the same cats. But for other people it may be different. Great poets, great writers, they may not need to walk by the same streets. They may walk by different streets and yet do the same things. This difference may not be due to efforts but to capacities, to achievement and to scope of thinking and feeling. A great poet may not need to write the same verses again. Perhaps he got not all, but sufficient, out of his environment, so that he may try something else that he did not try the last time.

'After hearing the lectures, people always ask if great poets have the being of man 1, 2 and 3. Now you say that a poet need not do the same thing over again.'

No. He may be a great poet and yet not belong to objective art. Others less great may produce objective art.

Think about some of these ideas, but do not think that you know. There are many variations, many possibilities. Think, because there is nothing more important for you.

2

Surface Personality

*

A Study of Imaginary Man

Foreword

The text of this chapter is a reconstruction of things said by P. D. Ouspensky at meetings held between 1930 and 1944. A few verbal changes have been inevitable in trying to bring together and make a sequence of replies to questions in differing contexts; but care has been taken not to change or add anything to the author's meaning. Questions asked by members of Ouspensky's groups are set within quotation marks, to distinguish them from Ouspensky's words which are not set within quotation marks.

There are words and expressions in this book which have special meanings in connection with a system of the Fourth Way which Ouspensky taught. The book cannot be understood by anyone who does not know these meanings. No explanation is attempted here, first because this book is intended for people who know the language already, and secondly because explanations of the special terms can be found in Ouspensky's published works, in particular, *The Psychology of Man's Possible Evolution* (New York, 1950 *and* London, 1951).

Summary of Contents

Development of conscience the aim of this system 53. Buffers an obstacle to development of conscience 53. Necessity of moral sense 53. Buffers and conscience 54-6. Meaning of 'soul' in this system 56. Soul feeds the moon 56. Creating moon in oneself 57-8. Plurality of our being and absence of permanent 'I' 58. Finding what can be changed in oneself by making a division between 'I' and the rest 58-60. Five meanings of the word 'I' 60. False personality 61. Essence and personality and their relation to fate and accident 61-6. Laws and influences 66. Study of false personality, as a means of learning to self-remember 67-70. False personality and negative emotions 70-1. Learning to know false personality and finding the chief feature of it 71-5. Right division of oneself 75-6. Danger of becoming two 76. Crystallization 76. False personality defends itself 78. Static triad 79-85. Valuation 85-6.

1

The aim of this system is to bring man to conscience. Conscience is a certain quality that is in every normal man. It is really a different expression of the same quality as consciousness, only consciousness works more on the intellectual side and conscience more on the moral (i.e. emotional) side. Conscience helps a man to realize what is good and what is bad in his own conduct. Conscience unites the emotions. We can experience on the same day a great many contradictory emotions, both pleasant and unpleasant, on the same subject, either one after another or even simultaneously, and we do not notice the contradictions because of the absence of conscience. Buffers are what prevent one 'I' or one personality from seeing another, but in a state of conscience a man cannot help seeing all these contradictions. He will remember that he said one thing in the morning, another thing in the afternoon and yet another in the evening, but in ordinary life he will not remember, or — if he does — he will insist that he does not know what is good and what is bad.

The way to conscience is through destroying buffers, and buffers can be destroyed through self-remembering and through not identifying.

The idea of conscience and the idea of buffers need long study, but when speaking about the moral side of this system, what should be understood from the beginning is that a man must have a sense of good and bad. If he has not, nothing can be done for him. He must start with a certain moral sense, a sense of right or wrong, in order to get more. He must understand first the relativity of ordinary morality, and secondly he must realize the necessity of objective right and wrong. When he realizes the necessity of objective permanent right and wrong, then he will look at things from the point of view of this system.

Conscience is in the essence, not in personality, whereas magnetic centre is in personality, not in essence. Magnetic centre is acquired in this life. It is in the intellectual part of emotional centre, though perhaps also in the intellectual part of the intellectual centre, and it is built on B influences.

'To awaken conscience does one not have to eliminate buffers?' someone asked.

When buffers are only shaken, conscience awakes.

'How can one discover what one's own buffers are?' asked someone else.

Sometimes it is possible. If one has the right idea of buffers, one may find one's own.

There is a great difference between excuses and buffers. Excuses may be different every time, but if the excuse is always the same, then it becomes a buffer.

Buffers are connected with conscience. Conscience is a word we use generally in a conventional sense, to mean a sort of educated emotional habit. Really, conscience is a special capacity which everybody possesses but which nobody can use in the state of sleep. Even if we feel conscience for a moment accidentally, it will be a very painful experience, so painful that immediately we shall want to get rid of it. People who have occasional glimpses of conscience invent all kinds of methods to get rid of this feeling. It is the capacity to feel at the same time all that we ordinarily feel at different times. Try to understand that all our different 'I's have different feelings. One 'I' feels that he likes something, while another hates it, and a third 'I' is indifferent. But we never feel these things at the same time because between them are buffers. Because of these buffers we cannot use conscience, cannot feel at the same time two contradictory things which we feel at different times. If a man does happen to feel them he suffers. So, in our present state, buffers are even necessary things without which a man would go mad. But if he understands about them and prepares himself, then after some time, he may start to destroy the contradictions and break the buffers down.

The breaking of a mechanical habit, whether good or bad, may be uncomfortable, because we have mechanical habits such as rules of conduct and moral rules which we get from our education. In most cases, therefore, we do not experience conscience; we have too many buffers. As I have said, they are partitions between our emotional attitudes, and experience of conscience means seeing a hundred things at the same time. Partitions disappear and all inner contradictions are seen at the same time. This is very unpleasant, and as the general principle of life is to avoid unpleasant sensations and realizations we run away from seeing them. In this way we create inner buffers. Contradictions seen one after the other do not appear contradictory; they have to be seen at the same time.

We are machines and we must see where we can change something, because in every machine of every kind there is always a point where it is possible to begin.

Sometimes people ask if there is anything permanent in us. There are two things, buffers and weaknesses. The weaknesses are sometimes called features, but they are really just weaknesses. Everyone has one, two or three particular weaknesses, and everybody has certain buffers belonging to him. He consists of buffers, but some are particularly important because they enter into all his decisions and all his understandings. These features and buffers are all that can be called permanent in us, and it is lucky for us that there is nothing more permanent, because these things *can* be changed.

Buffers are artificial; they are not organic; they are

acquired chiefly by imitation. Children begin to imitate grown-up people and so they create some of their buffers. Others are created unknowingly by education. If it were possible to put a child amongst people who were awake he would not fall asleep, but — in the conditions in which we live — imaginary personality or imaginary 'I' generally appears in a child at the age of seven or eight. Sometimes people ask whether we can see buffers in our present state of consciousness. We can see them in other people, but not in ourselves.

2

Man is divided into four parts: body, soul, essence, and personality.

Personality and essence do not appear to be separate, but we can study what belongs to essence and what belongs to personality. The idea of the soul as a separate organism controlling the physical body cannot be said to be based on anything. The nearest approach to the idea of the soul as it was understood up to the seventeenth century is what is called essence. The term soul is used in this system, but in the sense of life-principle only. Essence, personality and soul, taken together, correspond to what used to be called soul. But the soul was supposed to have a separate existence from the body, whereas in this sytem we do not suppose essence, personality and soul to have a separate existence from the body.

We are told that when a man dies or when anything dies (man or cockroach, it is just the same) its soul (i.e. life-principle) goes to the moon. The soul is material; a certain quantity of fine matter, energy if you like, which leaves the body at death. In a normal man the soul has no consciousness, it is just mechanical so that it does not suffer. But man can create a sort of half-consciousness which can pass to the soul and then the soul going to the moon may be aware of what happens to it. This occurs only in some very rare cases and when essence has died during life. Then the soul can get some material from essence in this way. Actually there are many other people who kill essence and are really dead in life, but that does not concern us. So let us speak about what it would mean to create moon in oneself.

First, what is the moon? What is the moon's function in relation to man, individual man? What would happen if this function of the moon were to disappear; would it be beneficial or the opposite? We know, for instance, that the moon controls all our movements, so that if the moon were to disappear we should not be able to make any movements, we should collapse like marionettes whose strings had been cut.

We must realize that all this refers to *Being*. What are the features of our being? The chief feature of our being is that we are many, not one. If we want to work on our being, to make it correspond better to our aim, we must try to become one. But this is a very far aim. What does it mean to become one? The first step, which is still very far, is to create a permanent centre of gravity. This is what is meant by creating moon in ourselves. The moon is a permanent centre of gravity in our physical life. If we create a centre of gravity in ourselves, we do not need the moon.

But first we must decide what the absence of permanent 'I' means. We shall find in its place many of the features or weaknesses referred to above, but these must be established definitely, for ourselves, by observation. Then we must begin a struggle against these features which prevent us from becoming one. We must struggle with imagination, negative emotions and self-will. Before this struggle can be successful we must realize that the worst possible kind of imagination from the point of view of obtaining a centre of gravity is a belief that one can *do* anything by oneself. After that we must strive with the negative emotions which prevent us from doing what we are told in connection with this system. For it is necessary to realize that self-will can only be broken by doing what one is told. It cannot be broken by doing what one decides oneself, for that will still be self-will. Self-will is always struggle against another will. Self-will cannot manifest without opposing itself to another will.

It may be useful for you to take a piece of paper and to write on it what constitutes your being. Then you will see that being cannot grow by itself. For instance, one feature of our being is that we are machines; another, that we live in only a small part of our machine; a third, our plurality of 'I's. We say 'I' but this 'I' is different at every moment. At one moment I say 'I' and it is one 'I'; five minutes later I say 'I' and it is another 'I'. So we have many 'I's all on the same level and there is no central 'I' in control. This is the state of our being; we are never one and we are never the same. If you write down all these features you will see what would constitute a change of being and what can be changed. In each particular feature there is something that can change, and a little change in one feature means also a change in another.

One of the first and most important factors in trying to change oneself is the division of oneself. The right division is between what is really 'I', and all the rest which we can call 'Ouspensky', or whatever your name happens to be. If this division is not made, if one forgets about it and continues to think of oneself in the usual way, or if one continues to use 'I' and 'Ouspensky', but in the wrong way work stops. The first line of work can only make progress on the basis of this division. No other lines are open if this division is forgotten, but it must be the right division. It happens often that people make a wrong division. What they like in themselves they call 'I' and what they dislike, or what is weak or unimportant, this they call 'Ouspensky', 'Petroff', 'Ivanoff' or whatever their name happens to be. If they divide in this way it is quite wrong. It is not enough that you make a right division today and forget it tomorrow. You must make a right division and keep it in your memory.

[An actual example of wrong division was given. A man called Petroff who had belonged to one of Ouspensky's groups made a division of himself into two parts. One of these he described as 'keeping him alive' and called it 'I'; the rest he called Petroff.]

This wrong division is simply lying, lying to oneself which is worse than anything because the moment one meets with the smallest difficulty it will show itself by inner arguing and wrong understanding.

'What is the origin of this difficulty in dividing oneself?' asked Mrs X.

The origin is you and Mrs X. Mrs X. thinks she knows better than you do. She thinks she is more important and wishes you to do as she wants.

'One of the difficulties,' said Mr Y., 'is that Y. knows better than 'I' in certain situations.'

Y. knows nothing.

'But he thinks he does,' said Mr Y.

Do you have to obey? If you think he knows best, simply study him and this will bring you to the right understanding. The first condition is that you must believe nothing. What is the use of trying to create permanent 'I' while you continue to believe in Mr Y? The real 'I' is created by the desire *to be* and *to know* and the rest is non-existent. So really there is nothing to divide. We must believe nothing or we cannot come to anything.

In this system the word 'I' can be spoken of in five ways on five different levels. Man in his ordinary state, is a multiplicity of 'I's; this is the first meaning. In the diagram it is indicated by the square of 'I's. When a man decides to work, an observing 'I' appears (shown in black on the diagram); this is the second meaning. The third meaning, indicated by the smallest circle, is where Deputy Steward appears. He has control over a number of 'I's. The fourth meaning, indicated by the middle circle, is where the Steward appears. He has control over all 'I's. The fifth meaning is that of the Master. He is drawn as the big circle outside as he has Time-body. He knows the past and also the future, although there must be different degrees of this.

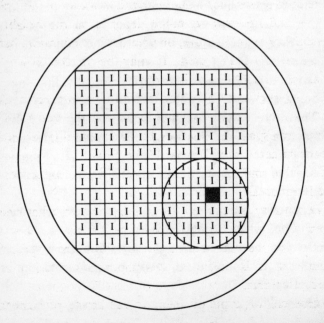

3

In this system, as has been explained, we make a division into 'I' and 'Jones', 'I' and 'Smith', and so on, whatever our names happen to be. What must now be understood is that Jones, Smith, Ivanoff, Petroff, and so on are the *False Personality* which each one of us has, but this division must not be confused with the division between Essence and Personality.

Essence is what we are born with, our capacities and incapacities. It is connected with 'type' and also with the physical body. We cannot work on it directly. From the point of view of work on ourselves, all that we have is personality. When a man begins to work, magnetic centre brings observing 'I' into being. This 'I' is also a personality which has to educate the rest of personality and essence.

'Is it right to suppose that a person with a highly developed personality would find this work more difficult?'

Yes and no. Not so much depends on the weight of personality as on its state, on whether it is educated, badly educated or uneducated. It may be in the power of imaginary 'I' and then it is wrong.

Being does not enter into the division into personality and essence. Knowledge and being are the two sides of which we speak in relation to the possibility of man's development. They make one pair of opposites. Personality and essence make another pair of opposites on a different scale.

Personality is acquired; essence is our own, what we are born with, what cannot be separated from us. They are mixed and we cannot distinguish the one from the other now, but it is useful to remember this division as a theoretical fact.

Essence, or type of man, is the result of planetary

influences. Planetary influences determine many big events in the life of humanity such as wars and revolutions. Our emotions come originally from the planets and different combinations of planetary influences create different essence. According to our type we act in one or another way in certain circumstances. It is said that there are twelve or eighteen chief types and then combinations of these. It is very seldom that you meet a pure type, but different features play a different part in different types, though each type has everything.

'If you were born of a certain type, could you ever change it?' somebody asked.

If it is a very bad type and you work very hard, you can change it. First you must know the type — that means knowing essence. If you find something in essence which is incompatible with aim, then if you work very hard you can perhaps change it. Essence is hidden in personality; rays of planetary influence cannot penetrate because personality is accidental. People are affected by planetary influences only in certain parts of themselves, parts which are always there, so that these influences have an effect on people in the mass but, in normal cases, seldom affect individuals.

'To what extent,' someone asked, 'does a man who is under the Law of Accident come under the Law of Fate, apart from his birth and death?'

It depends upon the relation between personality and essence. If personality is strong it makes a shell round essence, then there is very little fate. The planetary influences which control fate, type, essence, do not reach us when personality is very strong. But there are some people who, quite without the influence of 'schools', live more in essence. In them personality is very faint and they are more under the Law of Fate than other people. They depend more upon certain influences on which other people depend less; I will not say what these influences are, for that only leads to imagination. You must find out for yourselves. In the lives of ordinary people there is nothing of fate except birth and death. As I have said, individual man is very little under planetary influences because his essence is undeveloped and very small, or else too much mixed with his personality. As these influences cannot penetrate personality, such men are under the Law of Accident. If man lived in his essence he would live under planetary influences or, in other words, under the Law of Fate. Whether this would be to his advantage or not is another question. It might be better in one case and worse in another. Generally better. But planetary rays cannot penetrate personality; they are reflected from it.

[Replying to a question about planetary influences and astrology, Ouspensky said:]

Combinations of influences produce combinations of types. We do not know what they are and we cannot find out by making a horoscope. That would be something like mediaeval psychoanalysis.

'But the combinations do come from the planets, do they not?'

Yes, originally. All our emotions and all our ideas came originally from the planets, they were not born here.

'Should one try to live according to one's emotions, or should one always try to find a good reason for what one is doing?'

It is difficult to say. Emotions may be different and one's capacity to control one's life may be different. Very often it is imaginary. Very often all questions such as 'Should I do this?' or 'Should I do that?' are quite artificial, because one can *do* only in one way. Very often one thinks one can do something in this way or in that

way, but really one can only do it in one way. One has no
control. But, coming to the question itself, I think it is
useful to start from this point of view: to see what kind of
emotions you mean, whether they are emotions belonging
to essence or emotions belonging to personality. And very
often — not always, but very often — you can trust
emotions belonging to essence and mistrust emotions
belonging to personality. But this is not a general rule; it
only shows lines of study in connection with your
question. The question itself shows by which line your
thinking must go. You must think about essence and
personality. You must think about things that you can
control in yourself and things that you cannot control.
It is not a question for answer but for investigation.

'Is essence always good?'

No, not at all.

Essence is mechanical, it does not live by itself, it has
no special thinking apparatus; it has to think through
personality.

Essence, type and fate are practically the same, but facts
connected with fate are very difficult to find, except
perhaps just almost physical facts such as kind of health,
capacities or similar things. There are many other things
but they are hard to distinguish because in our state
essence seldom works separately from personality. Many
things that we have the inclination to ascribe to fate really
belong to personality. So it is dangerous to draw
conclusions. But there are some things we can see, for
instance that certain types of people attract certain types
of people. They have the same kinds of friends, the same
kinds of troubles, the same kinds of difficulties, but, of
course, never without personality taking some part. So you
cannot call it pure fate; it is more like cause and effect.

'Must one work harder to alter one's type than to alter

acquired personality?'

If it is necessary, but perhaps the type is quite all right. In most cases it is personality that must be changed; uncontrolled personality cannot be right.

Only very few people can work on essence. It is not exactly an advantage to the people who can, because it is very difficult for them. Generally we work on personality, and this is the only work we can do, and if we work it will bring us somewhere.

'When we try to change our being is essence as much affected as personality?'

We have to work on personality but essence is affected if we really change something.

'Did you say that personality is all lies?'

No, I said that personality was almost all artificial, just as essence is almost all real.

'Are our 'I's part of personality or essence?'

Both. There are 'I's belonging to essence and 'I's belonging to personality.

'Are they connected with different centres?' continued the same questioner.

Certainly, there are intellectual 'I's, moving 'I's and instinctive 'I's.

An 'I' is just one desire, one wish. But this distinction is only for convenience. You may forget it if you like, although it is like that. Just take it that 'I's are small and personality is already more complicated desires.

'Is the instinctive centre closely connected with one's essence?'

Yes, it controls the necessitites of essence.

'Is intelligence part of essence?'

Generally speaking, yes. But I would like to know what you mean by intelligence. If I say 'yes' you cannot apply it; it will remain dead capital.

'Can intelligence grow or increase by certain treatment?' asked the same questioner.

That is what I said. If we speak about ourselves, we shall see that intelligence belongs to essence and personality in a very mixed way; though, in a cosmic way, a certain amount of intelligence is given to every essence.

4

Man lives under a great many laws — physical, physiological, biological, laws created by man himself and so on, until we come to the laws of personal life and finally to imaginary 'I'. This is the most important law which governs our life and makes us live in the non-existing seventh dimension. A great many forces or influences act on a man at any given moment, though people are chiefly controlled by imagination. We imagine ourselves to be different from what we are and that creates illusions. But there are necessary laws. We are limited to certain food and to certain air, to a certain temperature and so on. We are so conditioned by influences that we have very little possibility of freedom. It is necessary for us to change our inner attitude.

People who live exclusively under A influences and who take B influences, if they meet them, on the same level as A influences, usually die in this life. They may be physically alive but that does not mean that their essence can develop.

'Do dead people look like everyone else? Do they live as we live?'

Quite, yes. Because they have soul and the remains of essence. They can insure themselves!

'You spoke previously of creating permanent "I". What

do you mean by that?'

I mean that when you say 'I' you can be sure that it is the same 'I' each time. Now you say, 'I want this' and half an hour later you say, 'I want that'. The 'I' is quite different. There is one thing — *you* — and there are many imaginary 'I's. *You* is what really is, and you must learn to distinguish it. It may be very small, very elementary, but you can find something definite and permanent and sufficiently solid in yourself.

If you remembered all that has been said, you would remember yourself at the end of ten weeks. For instance, take the study of false personality. This is one of the quickest methods. The more you understand false personality the more you will remember yourself. What prevents self-remembering is, first of all, false personality. False personality cannot and does not wish to remember itself, and it does not wish to let any other personality remember. It just tries to stop self-remembering; takes some form of sleep and calls that self-remembering. Then it is quite happy.

False personality is something special; *you* are opposed to it. False personality must be made to disappear or, at any rate, it must not enter into this work. This applies to everybody and everybody must begin in this way. First of all you must know your false personality and you must not trust it in any way — its ideas, its words, its actions. You cannot destroy it but you can make it passive for some time, and then little by little you can make it weaker.

False personality does not really exist but we imagine that it exists. It exists by its manifestations but not as part of ourselves. Do not try to define it or you will lose your way in words, but it is necessary to deal with facts. Negative emotions exist but at the same time they do not exist; there is no real centre for them. This is one of the misfortunes of our state. *We are full of non-existent things.*

[Someone said that he sometimes doubted the genuineness of his interest in the work; he might be lying to himself. Ouspensky answered:]

Only you can answer that, and only if you do not forget the fundamental principles by saying 'I' about something when it is only one 'I'. You must get to know other 'I's and remember about them. If you forget this you forget everything. So long as you remember this you may remember everything. Forgetting about this is the great danger, and one slight change in something is sufficient to make everything wrong.

Some groups of 'I's are useful, some are artificial and some are pathological. All people play roles; each person has about five or six roles which he plays in his life. He plays them unconsciously, or if he tries to play them consciously, he identifies with them very soon and continues to play them unconsciously. These roles together make the imaginary 'I'.

False personality is imaginary 'I'.

[Somebody asked whether higher states of consciousness could produce more thoroughly bad people or more thoroughly good people equally. Ouspensky answered:]

No, that is wrong. Bad people can be produced only by increase of mechanicalness. Self-remembering cannot produce wrong results provided the connection is kept between it and other ideas of the system, but if one omits one thing and takes another thing from the system — for instance, if one seriously works on self-remembering without knowing about the idea of division of 'I's, so that one takes oneself as one (as a unity), from the beginning — then self-remembering will give wrong results and may even produce wrong crystallization and make development impossible. There are schools for instance or systems which, although they do not formulate it in this way, are actually based on false personality and on struggle *against* conscience. Such work must certainly produce wrong results. First it will create a kind of strength, but it will make the development of higher consciousness an impossibility. False personality either destroys or distorts memory.

Self-remembering is a thing which must be based on right function. At the same time you must work on the weakening of false personality. Several lines of work are suggested and explained from the beginning and all must go together. You cannot just do one thing and not do another. All are necessary for creating this right combin-ation, but first must come the understanding of and struggle with false personality. Suppose one tries to remember oneself and does not want to make efforts against false personality, then all its features will come into play, saying, '*I* dislike these people; *I* do not want this, *I* do not want that', and so on. Then it will not be work but quite the opposite. If one tries to work in this wrong way it can make one stronger than one was before but in such a case the stronger one becomes, the less is the possibility of development. Fixing before development − that is the danger.

'Is a bored man free from identification?'

Boredom is identification with oneself, with false personality, with something in oneself. Identification is an almost permanent state for us. It is the chief manifest-ation of false personality, and because of this we cannot get out of the false personality. You must be able to see this state apart from yourself, separated from yourself, and that can only be done by trying to become more conscious, trying to remember yourself, trying to be aware of yourself. Only when you become more aware of yourself are you able to struggle with manifestations like identification and lying, and with false personality itself. All work has to be on false personality. If you do any other work and leave this, it is useless work and you will fail very soon. As with negative emotions, lying and all imagination, false personality cannot exist without identification. You must understand that false personality is a combination of all lies, features and 'I's which can never be useful in any sense or in any way, either in life or in the work — like negative emotions.

'Is false personality entirely based on negative emotions?'

There are many things besides negative emotions in false personality. For instance, in false personality there are always bad mental habits — wrong thinking. False personality, or parts of false personality, is always based on wrong thinking. At the same time, if you were to take negative emotions away from false personality it would collapse; it could not exist without them.

'So all negative emotions spring from false personality?' asked someone else.

Yes, certainly. How could it be otherwise? False personality is so to speak a special organ for negative emotions, for displaying negative emotions, enjoying negative emotions, producing negative emotions. You remember that I said that there is no real centre for negative emotions. False personality acts as a centre for negative emotions.

'How can one deal with the conceit of false personality?'

You must know all its features first and then you must think rightly. When you think rightly you will find ways to deal with it. You must not justify it; it lives on justification, even glorification of all its features. At almost every moment of our life, even in quiet moments, we are always justifying it, considering it legitimate and finding all possible excuses for it. This is what is meant by wrong thinking. So first of all you must know false personality, and then you must think rightly about it. You must know what it is — place it so to speak — this is the first step. And, as I have said, you must realize that *all* identification, *all* considering, *all* lies, *all* lies to oneself, *all* weakness, *all* contradictions seen and unseen, *all these* are false personality. In addition, all forms of self-will belong to false personality, so sooner or later you have to sacrifice them.

'Did you say that *all* our likes and dislikes are in false personality?'

Most of them are. And even those which did not belong to it originally, which have real roots, all pass through false personality.

[Somebody asked if one had to know the whole of false personality in order to struggle against it because it seemed to him that one could only know little bits of it. Ouspensky answered:]

One must know it. It is like a special breed of dog. If you do not know it you cannot speak about it. If you have seen it you can speak about it. To see only bits, as you say, is quite enough. Every small part of it is of the same colour. If you see this dog once you will always know it. It barks in a special way; it walks in a special way.

[Somebody asked whether 'Chief Feature' (i.e. the chief feature of false personality) was a food for false personality. Ouspensky said:]

Chief feature is not food. Chief feature *is* false personality. False personality in most cases is based on one feature which enters into everything. Some day we will take some examples of chief feature and you will see how it is really that which makes false personality.

'What is the best way to look for one's chief feature?' someone asked.

Simply see yourself. I do not know how to explain it better. It is possible one may find something — chief feature of the moment. It is imaginary personality; this is chief feature for everybody.

'Can one alter one's chief feature?' asked someone else.

First it is necessary to know it. If you know it, much will depend on the quality of your knowing. If you know it well, then it is possible to change it.

'When an attitude at the back of a negative emotion is very old and habitual, possibly a feature, how can I attack it?'

Begin from the feature. Find the feature, talk about it and so on.

It is necessary to *think* about false personality and in some cases you can see definitely a kind of chief feature coming into everything, like the axis round which everything turns. It can be shown, but the person will say, 'Absurd, anything but not that!' Or sometimes it is so obvious that it is impossible to deny it, but with the help of buffers one can forget it again. I have known people who gave a name to their chief feature several times and remembered it for some time. Then I met them again and they had forgotten, or when they remembered they had one face, and when they had forgotten they had another face and began to speak as though they had never spoken about it at all. You must come near to it yourself. When you feel it yourself, then you will know; if you are only told, you may always forget.

'Can I get a clue to false personality by thinking of events in the past?'

Sometimes you may. Either in the past or in your friends. But you must understand that you also have false personality, not only your friends!

'Can we see false personality without help?'

There is nothing against it theoretically, only I never saw such a case and nobody else I know saw such a case. Even with help people are not generally prepared to see it. It is as if you were to show a man his reflection in a real, actual mirror, and he were to say, 'This is not me. This is an artificial mirror, not a real mirror. This is not a reflection of me.' But if a man is prepared, it is sometimes possible to recognize a feature of weakness in oneself. If a man knows this feature, if he begins to keep it in mind and to remember it, then there may be a certain moment when he is free from this feature, when his action is not determined by this weakness.

Sometimes our features or weaknesses take simple forms like laziness, but in other cases their forms are so well disguised that there are no ordinary words to describe them, and they can only be described by some kind of diagram or drawing.

Laziness is for some people three-quarters of their lives or more. Sometimes laziness is very important, sometimes it is the chief feature of false personality. Very often it is chief feature, and all the rest depends on laziness and serves laziness. But remember that there are different kinds of laziness. It is necessary to find them by observing yourself and observing other people. For instance, there are very busy people who are always doing something and yet their *minds* may be lazy. That happens more often than anything else. Laziness is not only the desire to sit and do nothing.

[At one of his meetings somebody asked Ouspensky whether one could do anything by oneself or whether it must be done with the help of others. Ouspensky said that when he told people what should be done they immediately began to argue, and not only argue but they became negative. He said that that was really why help could not be given, and why it was necessary to make rules and definite demands. If all that was needed were just to show people what to do, that would be simple, but it was not always easy to explain the chief feature of false personality.] Sometimes it is seen clearly, at other times it is more hidden and difficult to see, and then it is only possible to think in a general way of false personality. But there was not a single case where I showed chief feature when people did not start violent arguing.

[At another meeting somebody said that he was occasionally able to observe himself in the act of considering or becoming identified. He asked whether in this way he might come to know his false personality, and by observing it to weaken it. Ouspensky answered that this was the only way and was very good so long as one did not get tired of trying to do it.] In the beginning, many people start very eagerly but soon get tired and begin to use the word 'I' indiscriminately, without asking themselves which 'I', which part of 'I'. Our chief enemy is the word 'I', because we have no right to use it really in ordinary conditions. Much later, after long work, we can begin to think of one of the groups of 'I's (like what has been called Deputy Steward) which develop from magnetic centre as 'I'. But in ordinary conditions when you hear yourself saying '*I* do not like', you must ask yourself which of your 'I's does not like. In this way you will remind yourself about the plurality which is in all of us. If you forget about it one time it will be easier to forget it next time. There are many good beginnings in the work and then this is forgotten and people start to slide down, and in the end all that happens is that they become more mechanical than before.

'Can we not find our features by observation?'

It is very improbable. We are too much in them; we do not have enough perspective, so that real work, serious work, begins only from feature. I do not mean that this is absolutely necessary for every individual because there are cases in which features cannot be defined. The definition would have to be so complicated that it would have no practical value. In such a case it is sufficient to take the general division between 'I' and 'Ouspensky'. Only, it is necessary to come to a *right* understanding of what is 'I' and what is 'Ouspensky', that is to say, what is you and what is lying. It is not sufficient, for instance, to admit this possibility of division and then to say that what you like is 'I' and what you dislike is not 'I'. It is long work and the right division cannot be found at once, but there must be some indications which you can find of the way in which to begin. For instance, suppose you formulate your aim in connection with this work by saying, 'I want to be free'. That is a very good definition, but then what is necessary? It is necessary to understand first of all that you are not free. If you understand to what extent you are not free, and if you formulate your desire to be free, then you will see in yourself which part of yourself wants to be free and which part does not want to be free.

[Somebody asked whether the fact of seeing a feature was in itself sufficient to diminish it, and also what one could put in its place. Ouspensky said that seeing did not diminish it, that it was necessary to work against it. He continued:] First one should try to check it by direct struggle. Suppose one finds that one argues too much, then one must not argue, that is all. Why put anything in its place? There is no need to put anything in its place except just silence.

[Somebody spoke about a useless personality which she enjoyed although she knew that it was useless. Ouspensky said:] In such a case you can struggle with this personality by strengthening other personalities opposed to it. Suppose you have a certain definite feature you want to struggle with, and try to find some other feature incompatible with it and which may be useful. If in your present equipment you find nothing sufficiently strong to put against it, look in your memory. Suppose you find some feature that is incompatible with the one you want to get rid of, and that can be useful, then just replace one by the other. But it may happen that even then they can both live happily together. One may be present in the evening, the other in the morning, and they may never meet.

There is only one real danger. If, for a long time, one goes on without making sufficient efforts or without doing anything seriously, then, instead of becoming one, one becomes divided into two so that all features and personalities are divided into two groups — one part useful to the work and helping personal work, and another part either indifferent or even unfriendly. This is a real danger because if two parts begin to form like this, the indifference of one spoils the result of the work of the other. So it is necessary to struggle very quickly and very strongly against that, otherwise it may lead to double crystallization.

'What do you mean by crystallizing?'

We use the word in a particular sense. Any feature may become crystallized just as buffers crystallize. This term came from the theosophical terminology; it is sometimes a useful term. I think everybody here has heard about higher bodies, the astral, mental and causal. The idea is that man has only one *physical* body, and development consists in the development of *higher* bodies. So man no. 5 corresponds to the crystallization of the astral body, man no. 6 to the crystallization of the mental body, and man no. 7 to the crystallization of the causal body.

But, speaking of the crystallization of features, one person may have very good and very beautiful features and yet behind them he may have one small feature of false personality which makes work very difficult for him, more difficult perhaps than it is for somebody else who has not got such brilliant features.

False personality may pretend to take an interest in the work, may take things for itself and call some negative and mechanical action 'self-remembering' or something of that sort. But it cannot do any useful work; it can only spoil the work of personalities which can do some work and get some results.

The system in the light of false personality is quite a different system; it becomes something that strengthens false personality and weakens the real system for you. The moment false personality takes the system to itself, it adds one word here and another word there. You cannot imagine how extraordinary some of these ideas are when they are repeated back to me. One word omitted from some formulation makes quite a different idea; and false personality is fully justified and can do what it likes and so on.

'Does our capacity for work increase just so much as we are able to weaken false personality?'

Everything one can get, one can get only at the expense of false personality. Later, when it is not present, one can get many things at the expense of other things, but for a long time one has to live, so to speak, off false personality.

'Is false personality the main barrier to being aware?'

First of all, yes. But many mechanical habits besides. Sometimes even mechanical habits in other centres.

'If you could eliminate false personality . . . ' someone began.

You cannot eliminate anything; it is just the same as trying to cut your head off. But you can make false personality less insistent and less permanent. If at a certain moment you feel the danger of the manifestation of false personality and you can find a way to stop it, this is what you have to begin with. The question of elimination does not enter at all; that is connected with quite different things. You must learn to control manifestations. But if people *think* that they can do something and at the same time refuse to *work* on acquiring this control, then things become bad for them. People can be enthusiastic about what they have to do until they know what they have to do. When they know, they become very negative and try to avoid it or explain it in some other way. This is what you must understand — that *false personality defends itself.* You must understand, too, that you cannot even begin to work such as you are, on your present level. First you have to change one thing or another thing. But you can only find out what to change as the result of your own observations, and it is different for different people. Sometimes it becomes quite clear what has to be changed and then the fight begins, because *false personality defends itself.* In order to struggle with false personality always do something which false personality does not like and you will very soon find out what it does not like. If you continue, it will get more and more irritated and will show itself more and more clearly, so that soon there will be no question about it. But if you do nothing to check false personality, it grows. It cannot diminish by itself. Tastes may change and so on, but it grows. This is the only development that happens in mechanical life — nothing else.

5

Let us speak about the relation of false personality to other parts of man. In every man at every moment, his development proceeds by what may be called a static triad. This triad is called a static triad because body, soul and essence always stay in the same place and act as the neutralizing force, while the other forces change only very slowly. So the whole triad is more or less in the same place all the time.

The first triangle shows the state of man in ordinary life; the second shows his state when he begins to develop. There are long periods between the state of the first and the state of the second triangle, and still longer between them and the third triangle. Actually, there are many intermediate stages but these three are sufficient to show the way of development in relation to false personality.

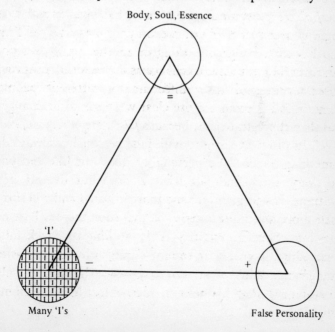

Body, Soul, Essence

=

'I'

−   +

Many 'I's   False Personality

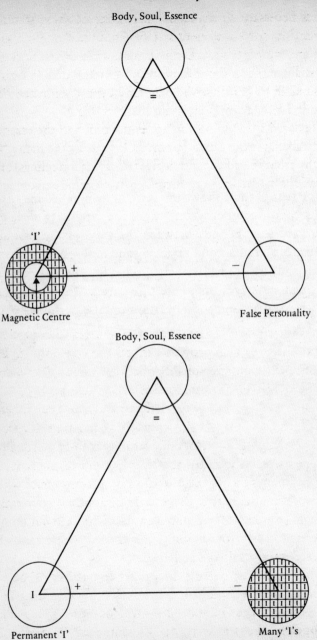

It is necessary to remember that none of these states is permanent. Any state may last for about half an hour and then another state may come, then again a different state. The diagram only shows *how* development goes. It would be possible to continue the diagram beyond permanent 'I', because permanent 'I' again has many forms.

The triad is made by the body, the soul and the essence at the apex. At the second point is 'I'; that is, the many 'I's which are the person, that is to say, all feelings and sensations which do not form a part of *false* personality.

The third point of the triangle is held by false personality (i.e. the imaginary picture of self).

In an ordinary man false personality calls itself 'I', but after some time, if a man is capable of development, magnetic centre begins to grow in him. He may call it 'special interests', 'ideals', 'ideas' or something like that. But when he begins to feel this magnetic centre in him, he finds a separate part of himself, and from this part his growth begins. This growth can take place only at the expense of false personality because false personality cannot appear at the same time as magnetic centre.

If magnetic centre is formed in a man he may meet a school, and when he begins to work he must work against false personality. This does not mean that false personality disappears; it only means that it is not always present. In the beginning it is nearly always present but when magnetic centre begins to grow it disappears, sometimes for half an hour, sometimes even for a day. Then it comes back and stays for a week! So all our work must be directed against false personality.

When false personality disappears for a short time, 'I' becomes stronger, only it is not really 'I', it is many 'I's. The longer the periods for which false personality disappears, the stronger the 'I' composed of many 'I's becomes. Magnetic centre may be transformed into deputy steward, and when deputy steward acquires control of false personality it really transfers all the unnecessary things to the side of false personality, and only the necessary things remain on the side of 'I'. Then, at a still further stage, it may be that permanent 'I' will come on the 'I' side with all that belongs to it. Then many 'I's will be on the false personality side, but we cannot say much about that now. There will be permanent 'I' with all that belongs to it, but we do not know what belongs to it. Permanent 'I' has quite different functions, quite a different point of view from anything we are accustomed to.

The static triad shows that either personal work or degeneration is going on in relation to different manifestations of false personality, but that body, soul and essence remain the same all the time. After some time they too will be affected, but they do not enter into the initial stages. Body will remain the same body, essence will change later, but it does not enter the beginning of the work. According to this system, essence enters only as much as it is mixed with personality. We do not take it separately because, as already explained (p. 56), we have no means of working on essence apart from personality.

'What is it', someone asked, 'that makes the real "I" begin to develop and false personality to fade?'

First of all it is a question of time. Say false personality in ordinary life is there for twenty-three hours out of every twenty-four, then when work begins it will be there for twenty-two hours only and magnetic centre will be present for an hour longer than usual. Then, in time, all false personality will diminish and will become less important. (This is shown in the second stage of the diagram where false personality has become passive and the many 'I's surrounding magnetic centre have become active.) You cannot diminish false personality in the sense of size but you can diminish it in the sense of time.

Somebody else said, 'I had the impression until now that false personality was the collection of all the many "I"s. This diagram has made things a little obscure to me.'

Among these many 'I's there are many passive 'I's which may be the beginning of other personality. False personality cannot develop; it is all wrong. That is why I said that all work has to be against false personality. If one fails it is because one has not given enough attention to false personality, has not studied it, has not worked against it. False personality is made up of many 'I's and they are all imaginary.

'I do not understand what you mean by passive "I"s.'

'I's which are controlled by some other, active 'I'. For instance, good intentions are controlled by laziness. Laziness is active, good intentions passive. The 'I' or combination of 'I's in control is active. The 'I's which are controlled or driven are passive. Understand it quite simply.

This diagram represents a state, then a slightly different state and again a different state. With the help of this diagram you can see three different states of man beginning from the most elementary. In the most elementary state false personality is active and 'I' is passive. Body, soul and essence always remain neutralizing. When, after many stages, permanent 'I' comes, then 'I' becomes active, many 'I's become passive and false personality disappears. Many different diagrams can be drawn between these two extremes, and further than that there are several possibilities.

[Ouspensky was asked whether there was a place in the static triad where a group of 'I's unconnected with magnetic centre was active and false personality passive. He answered that when he said that certain groups of 'I's or personalities became active, he meant those that were centred round magnetic centre.] First magnetic centre itself, and then those 'I's that range themselves round magnetic centre are opposed to false personality. Then, at a certain moment, magnetic centre becomes active and false personality passive. Magnetic centre is a combination of a certain group of interests. Magnetic centre does not lead you, for leading would mean progress and you remain in one place. But when things come, then with the help of magnetic centre you will be able to see which is which or whether you are interested or not interested in a thing. You can make a choice. Before one comes into the work, magnetic centre has reached a certain point which transforms it into a certain group of interests. When one meets the work it becomes interested in school-work and then it disappears as magnetic centre, because magnetic centre is a weak thing. This diagram is intended to describe the initial stages of the work and so I have put in very few of the combinations which might be shown. For instance, in the first triangle we have a triad composed of body, soul and essence (=), false personality (+), and 'I's (–). Now supposing that these 'I's are already divided into certain groups, then one of those groups is magnetic centre. Then there are other groups, maybe not attached, but still not hostile to the magnetic centre, which can exist and eventually develop into something better. The groups of 'I's which are always hostile and always harmful are false personality itself.

[Somebody asked whether the change from one form of the static triad to another depended on change of being.]

Yes, every small change is a change of being although this expression is generally applied to bigger, more serious changes. When we speak about change of being we speak about change from men nos 1, 2 and 3 to man no. 4 for instance. This is change of being, but of course this big jump consists of many small jumps. The static triad represents you. It shows the *state* of your being, what you are at a given moment. One of the points, body and essence, is always the same, but the relation of the other two points changes. If body and essence are normal they are impartial and do not take one side or the other, but if there is something wrong in them they are on the side of false personality.

6

When in a state of doubt remember to try and bring up other 'I's which have a certain valuation. This is the only way to conquer doubts. In order to develop you must have some capacity for valuation. The only practical approach is to think of the different sides of yourself and to find the sides that can work and the sides that cannot. Some people have real values, some have false values and some have no values at all. It is the same with different 'I's; some value real things, some wrong things and some value nothing.

People can spend their lives studying systems and system words and never come to real things. Three-quarters or nine-tenths of our ordinary knowledges does not really exist; it exists only in imagination.

Realization of sleep is the only one thing. It is necessary to find ways to awaken, but before that you must realize that you are asleep. Compare sleep and waking. All ideas of the work begin with the idea of sleep and the possibility of waking. All other ideas — life ideas — may be clever or elaborate but they are all ideas of sleeping people produced for other sleeping people. Sleep is the result of many things: division of personalities, different 'I's, contradictions, identifications and so on. But the first thing of all, just pure without any theory, is *the realization of sleep.*

3

Self-Will

*

A Compilation of things said
by P. D. Ouspensky mainly about
the need to subjugate Self-Will
as a preparation for the growth of Will

Foreword

The text which follows was put together from answers given to questions at meetings held by P. D. Ouspensky in London and New York between 1935 and 1944.

Although the material has not been arranged chronologically, care has been taken not to distort the sense of any of Ouspensky's answers by placing them beside other answers which belong to a different line of thought. Care has also been taken not to interfere with the intention of the answers by an over-shortening of the contexts from which they are taken. For this reason some of the principal ideas about struggle with self-will are repeated several times in the text in almost the same words.

Self-Will is intended for people who are familiar with the system taught by Ouspensky and its special terminology. Both the system and the language are described by P. D. Ouspensky in *The Psychology of Man's Possible Evolution* (New York, 1950 *and* London, 1951), and *In Search of the Miraculous* (New York, 1949 *and* London, 1950).

Summary of Contents

Changing being 90. The necessary condition 90. Understanding, work on emotions and will 90. Giving up will because we have no will 90. Moments of will 90. How to think about will 91. Man cannot 'do' 91. The law of accident 91. Everything happens 92. Change only possible with help of system and right instruments 92. 'Doing' begins by *not* doing 92–3. We must begin with aim 93. Self-remembering useless without aim 94. Self-will and wilfulness mistaken for will 94. Each 'I' has its own will 94. Will is the resultant of desires 95. Opposing self-will with work 95. How things happen: accident, cause and effect, fate, will 95. Struggle must be by will and intentional 96. Using the rudiments of will to make will grow 96. The far aim 96. Weakness and strength 96. Need for organized work 97. Three lines of work in oneself 97–8. Before we can change anything we must understand emotionally that everything happens and we must work beyond our forces 98. We cannot make decisions but if we find out how to make regular efforts and how to think rightly, we shall begin to see ourselves 99–101. Difference between will of ordinary men and will based on knowledge, consciousness and permanent 'I' 101. Determination and definition of aim 101. Bringing aim nearer 102. What is a good aim? 102. Aim must be practical and not too remote 103. We must know what we want and want in the right order 103. The first aim is to see onself 104. Necessary to work on being 104. Learning to control more than one centre 104–5. Struggle against self-will by remembering the work 105. Ordinary will described 106. Self-remembering is moments of will 107. Will and freedom 107. What giving up will means 107–10. Development cannot be mechanical 110. Nothing can be given 111. Everything must be paid for 111. *What* do we want and can we pay? 112. Moral action 112.

Ouspensky. Life is not long enough for changing our being if we work on it as we do at everything else in life. Something can be attained only if one uses a more perfected kind of method. The first condition is understanding. All the rest is proportionate to understanding. There must also be efforts in connection with emotions and will. One must be able to go against oneself to give up one's will.

First you must ask yourself: What is will? We have no will, so how are we to give up what we do not have? This means, first, that you never agree that you have no will; you only agree in words. Secondly, we do not always have will but only at times. Will means a strong desire. If there is no strong desire, there is nothing to give up; there is no will. At another moment, we have a strong desire that is against work, and if we stop it, it means that we give up will. It is not at every moment that we can give up will but only at special moments. And what does it mean 'against work'? It means against rules and principles of the work or against something you are personally told to do or not to do. There are certain general rules and principles, and there may be personal conditions for different people.

Question. Should one ask for further personal directions?

Ouspensky. Yes, but if one asks one must obey. One is not obliged to do anything if one does not ask, so before asking one must think twice.

Question. If one is prepared to obey, will you give directions?

Ouspensky. If opportunity offers. It must be at a moment when you have will. There must be a definite desire to do something that affects work or other people. Usually we have bad will. We very seldom have good will. If you have good will, I do not speak about it; I simply say, 'Go on, continue, learn'.

There are many things mixed here. You do not know how to think about will. With one side of you, you realize that you are machines, but at the same time you want to act according to your own opinion. In that moment you must be able to stop; not to do what you want. This does not apply to moments when you have no intention of doing anything, but you must be able to stop if your desire goes against rules or principles, or against what you have been told.

It is important to realize two things: that we cannot 'do' and that we live under the law of accident. In most cases people think they can 'do', that they can get what they want and that it is only accidental that they do not. People think that accident is very rare and that most things are due to cause and effect. This is quite wrong. It is necessary to learn to think in the right way, then we shall see that everything *happens* and that we live under the law of accident.

In relation to 'doing', it is difficult for us to realize, for example, that when people build a bridge, that is not 'doing'; it is only the result of all previous efforts. It is accidental. To understand this, you must think of the first bridge that Adam built and of all the evolution of bridges. At first it is accidental — a tree falls across a river, then man builds something like that, and so on. People are not 'doing'; one thing comes from another.

If you remember that you can *do nothing*, you will remember many other things. Generally there are three or four chief stumbling-blocks, and if you do not fall over one, you fall over another. 'Doing' is one of them. In connection with this, there are some fundamental principles which you must never forget. For instance, that you must look at yourself and not at other people; that people can do nothing by themselves, but — if it is possible to change — it is possible only with the help of the system, the organization, personal work and study of the system. You must find things like that and remember them.

Question. How can one make sure of remembering them?

Ouspensky. Imagine yourself starting to make plans to do something. It is only when you really try to do something *differently* from the way it *happens* that you realize that *it is absolutely impossible to do differently.* Half of the questions asked are about 'doing' — how to change this, destroy that, avoid this and so on. But enormous effort is necessary to change even one small thing. Until you try you can never realize it. You can change nothing except through the system. This is generally forgotten.

Everything happens. People can do nothing. From the time we are born to the time we die things happen, happen, happen, and we think we are 'doing'. This is our ordinary normal state in life, and even the smallest possibility to 'do' something comes only through the work, and first only in oneself, not externally. Even in oneself, 'doing' very often begins by *not* doing. Before you can do something that you cannot do, you must *not do* many things which you did before.

Question. Does one sometimes have a choice between two possible happenings?

Ouspensky. Only in very small things, and even then if you notice that things are going in a certain way and decide to change them, you will find how awfully uncomfortable it is to change things. So you come back to the same things.

Question. When one really begins to understand that one cannot 'do', one will need a great deal of courage. Will that come from getting rid of false personality?

Ouspensky. One does not come to this understanding just like that. It comes after some time of work on oneself, so that when one comes to this realization one has many other realizations besides; chiefly that there are ways to change if one applies the right instrument at the right place and at the right time. One must have these instruments, and these again are only given by work. It is *very* important to come to this realization. Without it one will not do the right things; one will excuse oneself.

Question. I do not understand why one should excuse oneself.

Ouspensky. One does not want to give up the idea that one can 'do', so that even if one realizes that things just happen, one finds excuses, such as, 'This is an accident but tomorrow it will be different'. That is why we cannot realize this idea. All our lives we see how things happen but we still explain them as accidents, as exceptions to the rule that we can 'do'. Either we forget, or do not see, or do not pay enough attention. We always think that at every moment we can begin to 'do'. This is our ordinary way of thinking about it. If you see in your life a time when you tried to do something and failed, that will be an example, because you will find that you explained your failure as an accident, an exception. If things repeat themselves, again you think you will be able to 'do', and if you see this again, again you will explain your failure as just an accident. It is very useful to go through your life from this point of view. You intended one thing and something different happened. If you are really sincere, then you will see; but if not, you will persuade yourself that what happened was exactly what you wanted!

Ouspensky. You must start with some concrete idea. Try to find what really prevents you from being active in work. It is necessary to be active in work; one can get nothing by being passive.

Now we forget the beginning, where and why we

started, and most of the time we never even think about *aim,* but only about small details. No details are of any use without aim. Self-remembering is of no use without remembering the aims of the work and the original fundamental aim. If these aims are not remembered emotionally, years may pass and one will remain in the same state. It is not enough to educate the mind; it it necessary to educate the will. You must understand what our will is. From time to time we have will. Will is the resultant of desires. The moment we have a strong desire, there is will. In that moment we must study our will and see what can be done. We have no will but self-will and wilfulness. If one understands that, one must be brave enough to give up one's will, to pay attention to what was said. You must look for those moments and you must not miss them. I do not mean create them artificially, although in a house [organized according to work principles] special possibilities to give up one's will are made, so that if you give up your will, later you may have your own will. But even people who are not in the house, if they watch themselves and are careful, can catch themselves at such moments, and ask themselves what they are to do. Everybody must find what is his own situation.

Question. How should we think about our inability to 'do' in relation to responsibilities?

Ouspensky. You are given certain definite tasks, things to do. When you learn to remember yourself, even a little, you will find you are in a better position in relation to all other things.

Question. Does the system put forward any thesis about will-power other than that by using it it grows, and by disuse it fades away?

Ouspensky. The system explains that you have many 'I's and that each has its own will. If instead of being many, you become one, then you will have one will. Will, in normal 1, 2 and 3 men, is only the resultant of desires. Certain conflicting desires, or combinations of desires, make you act in a certain way. That is all.

Question. Is the observing 'I' the embryo of Permanent 'I'?

Ouspensky. Observing 'I' is the embryo of Permanent 'I', but it has no real will. Its will is not opposed to self-will. What can be opposed to self-will? There are only two things opposed to one another: work and self-will. Self-will wants to talk, for instance, and there is a rule against talking. A struggle ensues, and the result is according to which of the two conquers.

Question. The making of effort is what you call struggle, but suppose one is not aware of a struggle?

Ouspensky. That means it happened. Things can happen to us in four ways — by accident, through cause and effect, by fate, and by will. Struggle must be by will, intention. And you must be aware of your intention. You cannot make effort and not be aware of it. Will would be if you wanted something, and decided and acted and achieved what you wanted. That is what is important.

Question. I thought I heard it said that if a man studies groups of 'I's, he will understand how groups of 'I's help each other.

Ouspensky. What is important in this case is will-action. At first we were told about three things only — will, fate, and accident. Then we came to the conclusion that there must be a fourth class corresponding to Karma. But as this word had gained many wrong associations from theosophy, we used the words 'cause and effect', meaning by them something that happens in this life and refers to oneself only, because from another point of view the whole world is based on cause and effect.

Question. In those four categories, will is not often used, is it?

Ouspensky. Will has to be used. We are never ready for work but we must work all the same. If we are ready, then we are given other work for which we are not ready.

Question. Knowing one's fate, how can one act along a line to avoid accident?

Ouspensky. I do not know what you mean by 'knowing fate'. It has nothing to do with avoiding accident. One avoids accidents (in our special sense) by creating causes and increasing effects. This is coming to will. It is not will but it is coming to it. Only a certain number of things can happen in an hour or a day, so if one creates more causes, there is less room for accidents to happen.

We can take fate only in relation to our physical state, to health and so on. Fate has nothing to do with attainment. Cause and effect begins it. But cause and effect is when the result depends on one's own action, but unpremeditated action. In work, one must try to use will — as much as we have of it. If one has one inch of will and uses it, then one will have two inches, then three, and so on.

Question. How can I learn to act differently in life so as to avoid the same limited and recurrent emotions which I now feel?

Ouspensky. This is our aim; this is the aim of the whole work. This is why work is organized, why we have to study different theories, to remember different rules, and so on. What you speak of is the far aim. We have to work in the system first. By learning how to act in connection with the system and the organization, we learn how to act in life; but we cannot learn how to act in life without first going through the system.

Question. If we are all weakness and no strength, from what source do we draw such strength as is needed even to begin work on ourselves?

Ouspensky. We must have certain strength. If we are only weakness, then we can do nothing. But if we had no strength at all, we should not have become interested in that work. If we realize our situation, we already have a certain strength, and new knowledge increases this strength. So we have quite enough to begin. Later, more strength comes from new knowledge and new efforts.

Ouspensky. Unless people make sufficient efforts from the beginning the system will be useless to them. Efforts must be organized. What does this mean? Unless you understand our work, we shall not be able to help you. You can be helped only if you enter into our work. One must work on three lines. Before one can understand what this means in relation to the *work,* one must understand three different lines of work in *oneself*: intellectual work (acquisition of knowledge), emotional work (work on emotions), and work on will (work on one's action). One has no big will such as man no. 7 has but one has will at certain moments. Will is the resultant of desires. Will can be seen at moments when there is a strong desire to do or not to do something. Only those moments are important. The system can help only those who realize that they cannot control their will. Then the system will either help them to control their will, or they will have to do as they are told.

Question. Is there no such thing as forcing a situation?

Ouspensky. It may look like that but really it happened. If it could not happen in that way, then it could not happen. When things happen in a certain way, we are carried by the current but we think that we control the current.

Question. If one feels for a moment that one is able to 'do', say, to put through a particular job in ordinary work, what is the explanation of that?

Ouspensky. If one is trained to do something one learns to follow a certain kind of happenings, or if you like, to start a certain kind of happenings, and then these develop, and one runs behind although one thinks one is leading.

Question. If one has the right attitude . . .

Ouspensky. No, attitude has nothing to do with it. Attitude may be right and understanding may be right, but you still find that things happen in a certain way. Any ordinary things. It is very useful to try to remember instances where one tried to do something differently and to see how one always came back to the same thing even if one made a slight deviation — enormous forces driving one back to the old ways.

Question. When you said that we cannot help the same things happening, did you mean until our being is changed?

Ouspensky. I did not speak about work. I said it was necessary to understand that *by ourselves* we cannot 'do'. When this is sufficiently understood, you can think what it is possible to do: what conditions, what knowledge and what help are needed. But first it is necessary to realize that, in ordinary life, if you try to do something different, you will find that you cannot. When this is emotionally understood, only then is it possible to go further.

Question. If we are machines, how can we change our being?

Ouspensky. You cannot wait until you change. There is one very important principle in the work — you never have to work in accordance with your forces, but always beyond your forces. This is a permanent principle. In the work you always have to do more than you can. Only then can you change. If you do only what is possible, you will remain where you are. One has to do the impossible. You must not take the word 'impossible' on a big scale, but even a little means much. You have to do more than you can, or you will never change. This is different from life —

in life you only do what is possible.

Question. I want to find the way to make a decision to work from which I cannot draw back.

Ouspensky. This is one of our greatest illusions, that we can make decisions. It is necessary *to be* in order to make decisions because, as we are, one little 'I' makes decisions and another 'I' which does not know about it, is expected to carry them out. This is one of the first points we have to realize, that, as we are, we cannot make decisions even in small things — things just happen. But when you understand this rightly, when you begin to look for the causes, and when you find these causes, then you will be able to work and perhaps you will be able to make decisions, but for a long time only in relation to work, not to anything else.

The first thing you have to decide is to do your own work and to do it regularly, to remind yourself about it, not to let it slip away. We forget things too easily. We decide to make efforts — certain kinds of effort and certain kinds of observation — and then just ordinary things, ordinary octaves, interrupt it all and we quite forget. Again we remember and again we forget, and so on. It is necessary to forget less and to remember more. It is necessary to keep certain realizations, certain things that you have already realized and understood, always with you. You must try not to forget them.

The chief difficulty is *what* to do and *how* to make yourself do it. To make yourself think regularly, work regularly — this is the thing. Only then will you begin to see yourself, that is, to see what is more important and what is less important, where to put your attention and so on. Otherwise what happens? You decide to work, to do something, to change things — and then you remain just where you were. Try to think about your work, what you are trying to do, why you are trying to do it, what helps you to do it and what hinders you, both from outside and inside. It can also be useful to think about external events because they show you how much depends on the fact that people are asleep, that they are incapable of thinking rightly, incapable of understanding. When you have seen this outside, you can apply it to yourself. You will see the same confusion in yourself on all sorts of different subjects. It is difficult to think, difficult to see where to begin to think: once you realize this, you start to think in the right way. If you find your way to think rightly about one thing, that will immediately help you to think rightly about other things. The difficulty is that people do not think rightly about anything.

Ouspensky. What does it mean to work practically? It means to work not only on intellect but also on emotions and on will. Work on intellect means to think in a new way, creating new points of view, destroying illusions. Work on emotions means not expressing negative emotions, not identifying, not considering, and later on, also work on the emotions themselves. Work on will: what does it mean? What is will in men nos 1, 2 and 3? It is the resultant of desires. Will is the line of combined desires, and as our desires constantly change, we have no permanent line. So, ordinary will depends on desires, and desires can be very different; desire to do something and desire not to do something. Man has no will but only self-will and wilfulness.

We have to ask ourselves on what the will of man no. 7 could be based. It must be based on full consciousness, and this implies knowledge and understanding connected with objective consciousness and a Permanent 'I'. So three things are necessary: knowledge, consciousness, and Permanent 'I'. Only those people who have these three things can have real will; that means, a will that is independent of all else and only based on consciousness, knowledge and a Permanent 'I'.

Now ask yourselves on what self-will and wilfulness is based. It is always based on opposition. Self-will is when, for instance, someone sees that a man does not know how to do a thing and says he will explain, and the man says, 'No, I will do it myself'. Self-will springs from opposition. Wilfulness is much the same only more general. Wilfulness can be a kind of habit.

In order to study how to begin work on will, how to transform will, one has to give up one's will. This is a very dangerous expression if it is misunderstood. It is important to understand rightly what 'to give up one's will' means. The question is how to do it. First, one must try to connect and to co-ordinate thoughts, words and actions, with ideas, requirements and interests of the system. We have too many accidental thoughts which change the whole thing. If we want to be in the work, we must verify all our thoughts, words and actions from the point of view of work. Some of them can harm the work. So, if you want to work, you are not free any more; you must lose the *illusion* of freedom. The question is: Have we freedom? Have we something to lose? The only freedom we have is to do harm to the work and to people. By learning not to harm the work we learn not to harm ourselves; not to perform irresponsible, unconnected actions. So we do not give up anything real.

Ouspensky. The determination and definition of aim is a very important moment in the work. It usually happens that one defines one's aim quite rightly, in quite the right direction, only one takes an aim that is very far off. Then, with this aim in view, one begins to learn and to accumulate material. The next time one tries to define aim, one defines it a little differently, finding an aim that is a little nearer. The next time again a little nearer, and so on, until one finds an aim that is quite close — tomorrow or the day after tomorrow. This is really the right way in relation to aims, if we speak about them without definite words. But besides them, we can find many that have been mentioned definitely. 'To be one.' Quite right; very good aim. 'To be free.' How? Only when one acquires control of the machine. One may say, 'I want to be conscious'. Quite right. Another may say, 'I want to have will'. Very good. 'I want to be awake.' Also very good. These are all aims on the same line, only at different distances.

Question. I have come to the conclusion that most of my aims are too remote and I want to work more on the practical side.

Ouspensky. Yes, because before you can reach remote aims, there are many things you have to do here and now, and that is where this system differs from almost all other systems. Nearly all other systems begin at least ten thousand miles ahead and have no practical meaning; but this system begins in this room. That is the difference, and that is what must be understood first of all.

Again and again we must return to this question of what we want from the work. Do not use the terminology of the system but find what you yourself want. If you say you want to be conscious, that is all very good, but why? What do you want to get by being conscious? You must not think that you can answer this question immediately. It is very difficult. But you must keep coming back to it. And you must understand that before the time comes when you will be able to get what you want, you must know what it is. This is a very definite condition. You can never get anything until you know it and can say, 'I want this'. Then perhaps you may get it or perhaps you may not; but you can never get it unless you know what it is. Also, you must want things in the right order.

Question. What does this mean?

Ouspensky. One must study and understand the right order of possibility. This is a very interesting subject.

Question. Do you mean in the system?

Ouspensky. With the help of the system. But you can formulate it in your own way. You must be sincere with yourself. You must know exactly what you want, and then you will ask yourself: 'Will the system be able to help me to get it?' and so on. But it is necessary to know what you want.

We are never the same for two days in succession. On some days we shall be more successful, on others less. All we can do is to control what we can. We can never control more difficult things if we do not control the easy things. Every day and hour there are things that we could control and do not; so we cannot have new things to control. We are surrounded by neglected things. Chiefly, we do not control our thinking. We think in a vague way about what we want, but if we do not formulate what we want, then nothing will happen. This is the first condition, but there are many obstacles.

I have spoken about this question of aim because I advise you to think about it, to revise what you have already thought about aim, and to think how you would define your aim now after a study of these ideas. It is useless to define an aim that cannot be attained. But if you define an aim that you can hope to attain, then your work will be conscious, serious.

If I were asked about this, I would answer that what a

man can get, what can be promised to him on condition that he works, is that after some time of work he will see himself. Other things he may get, such as consciousness, unity, connection with higher centres, all come after this — and we do not know in what order they come. But we must remember one thing; until we get *this* — until we see ourselves — we cannot get anything else. Until we begin to work with this aim in view we cannot say that we have begun to work. So, after some time we must be able to formulate our immediate aim as being to see oneself. Not even to *know* oneself (this comes later), but to *see* oneself.

Ouspensky. Even knowledge and understanding cannot help if one does not work on being. If will does not grow at the same time, one can understand and not be able to do anything.

Question. You say that it is possible to understand and yet not be able to do anything about it?

Ouspensky. Yes, if from the beginning one did not start making serious efforts to develop will. If will remains undeveloped, then the development of understanding cannot help much. One can understand very much, but at the same time not be able to do anything about it.

Question. Is will part of being?

Ouspensky. Yes, the same as consciousness or understanding. Only if you work too much on understanding and disregard will, then instead of growing stronger, your will will become weaker, or will remain the same as it was. With our will — the will of men nos 1, 2 and 3 — we can only control one centre, using all the concentration possible for us. We can never control two or three centres, and yet centres are dependent on one another. Suppose that we decide to control one centre and, meanwhile, other centres go on by themselves, then they will immediately corrupt the centre that we want to control and bring it again to mechanical reaction.

Question. How can one attain this kind of will?

Ouspensky. That was explained in relation to 'stop' exercise.[1] Those who heard that lecture about 'stop' exercise may remember it. To control more than one centre is the basis of 'stop' exercise. This can only be done if you put yourself under some other will because your own will is insufficient. Sometimes it may be necessary to control four centres, and the maximum of your energy of will can only control one centre. So another will is necessary. This is why school discipline is necessary and school exercises.

Question. How can we work against self-will? Is it possible for us, as we are, to recognize the moments when we have real will?

Ouspensky. Not real will; we cannot have that. All we have is self-will and wilfulness, or small wills that change all the time. Real will is very far off; it is based on Permanent 'I', consciousness and individuality. We have not got it.

About how we can work against self-will: you can study the system. There are certain demands in the system; things you must not do or must do. For instance, you must not talk, because if you do, you will only tell lies. You cannot speak about the system before you know and understand it. In this way, from the very beginning, you meet with ideas of the work opposed to self-will. If you forget about the work, you are not working against self-will. The only way to struggle against self-will is to remember the work. It may be that at one moment the work does not enter at all, but at another moment it does

1 For a description of the 'stop' exercise, see P. D. Ouspensky: *In Search of the Miraculous* (New York, 1949 and London, 1950), pp. 351–6.

enter, and in that moment you can understand what giving up self-will means. Ask yourself: Is it right from the point of view of the work or not? This is struggle against self-will.

First it is necessary to understand what will is. We have no will; we only have self-will and wilfulness. Self-will is self-assertion. Wilfulness is going against something, against rules, and so on. Both include a kind of opposition to something and in that form they exist. Man has no original will which can exist without opposition, and which is permanent. That is why it is necessary to subjugate it. This subjugation trains it so that afterwards it can follow a definite line. When it becomes strong enough, it is no longer necessary to limit it. So will cannot be left as it is. Now it runs in all directions. It has to be trained, and in order to train will one has to do many unpleasant things.

In an ordinary man will follows a zigzag line or goes in a circle. Will shows the direction of efforts. Effort is our money. We must pay with effort. According to the strength of effort and the time of effort — in the sense of whether it is the right time for the effort or not — we obtain results. Effort needs knowledge, knowledge of moments when effort is useful. The efforts we can make are efforts of self-observation and self-remembering. When people hear about effort, they think about an effort of 'doing'. That would be lost effort or wrong effort, but effort of self-observation and self-remembering is right effort because it can give right results.

Question. Why did you say we must try to remember ourselves when it is most difficult?

Ouspensky. You know you must not do something. One part of you wants to do it. Then remember yourself and stop it. Self-remembering has an element of will in it. If it were just dreaming, 'I am, I am, I am,' it would not be anything. You must give a certain time simply to studying what remembering means, and what not remembering means, and what effect these have. Then you can invent many different ways to remember yourselves. But actually self-remembering is not an intellectual or abstract thing; it is moments of will. It is not thought; it is action. It means having increased control; otherwise of what use would it be? You can only control yourself in moments of self-remembering. The mechanical control which is acquired by training and education — when one is taught how to behave in certain circumstances — is not real control.

Question. Are we to understand that self-remembering means awareness?

Ouspensky. Not only awareness. It means also a certain capacity to act in a certain way, to do what you want. You see, in our logical way of thinking, according to logical knowledge, we divide consciousness from will. But consciousness *means* will. In the Russian language, for instance, 'will' is the same word as 'freedom'. The word 'consciousness' means a combination of all knowledge; as if you had all your knowledge before you at the same time. But consciousness also means will, and will means freedom.

Question. What does giving up will mean?

Ouspensky. Giving up childishness, inefficiency and lying.

Question. Does giving up self-will involve giving up your own judgement?

Ouspensky. It depends in what. What does giving up will mean? How can it be achieved? You have mistaken ideas about this. First you think of it as a final action: that you give up will and have no more will. This is an illusion because we have no such will to give up. Our wills last for about three minutes. Will is measured by time. If once we give up three minutes of will, tomorrow another three minutes will grow. Giving up will is a continuous process, not one action. A single action means nothing. A second mistake is not remembering certain principles to which you give up will, such as rules. For example, there is a rule that you should not talk about this system. The natural desire is to talk, but if you stop yourself, it means that you give up your will; that you obey this rule. There are many other principles to which you must give up your will in order to follow them.

Question. Does giving up one's will mean not to act without understanding?

Ouspensky. You see, this is another of your mistakes. You think that giving up will means *doing* something. This happens very seldom. In most cases you are told *not* to do something. There is a great difference in this. For instance, you want to explain to someone what you think of him, and you must not do it. It is a question of training. Will can be grown if a man works on himself and makes his will obey the principles of the work. Things that do not concern the work cannot be connected with it, but the more you enter into the work, the more things begin to touch upon the work. But this needs time.

When their chance comes and people are told to do something, or not to do something, they go against it for what seems to them the very best of reasons. So they miss their opportunity. Time passes, and later they may see that they have missed their opportunity, but it can no longer be replaced by anything. That is the penalty of self-will.

About this idea of giving up one's will: it must be repeated that men nos 1, 2 and 3 have no will, but only self-will and wilfulness. Try to understand what that means. Being wilful means that one wants to do or actually does something forbidden, simply because it is forbidden.

And an instance of self-will is when someone sees that you are trying to do something that you do not know how to do and wants to help you, but you say, 'No, I will do it myself'. These are the two types of will we have. They are based on opposition. Real will must depend on consciousness, knowledge and Permanent 'I'. Such as we are, we have not got it. All that we have is self-will and wilfulness. Our will is a resultant of desires. Desires may be very well hidden. For instance, a man may want to criticize someone and he calls it sincerity. But the desire to criticize may be so strong that he would have to make a really big effort to stop it, and a man cannot make real efforts by himself.

In order to create will, a man must try to co-ordinate his every action with ideas of the work; he must in every action ask himself: How will it look from the point of view of the work? Is it useful or harmful to me, or to the work? If he does not know, he can ask. If a man has been long in the work, there is practically not a single action that does not touch upon the work; there are not independent actions. In that way one is not free, in the sense that one cannot act foolishly and without discrimination. One *must* think before one acts. If one is not sure, one can ask. This is the *only* method by which will can be created, and for this method school organization is necessary. Without school one can do nothing.

Question. In speaking about will, you said that first it would be the will of other people and later our own will. How shall we come under the will of other people?

Ouspensky. When you come into contact with the second and third lines of work, you necessarily come into contact with the will of others.

Question. Is not stopping the expression of negative emotions more or less the same thing as giving up wilfulness?

Ouspensky. Why do you want to translate one thing into another? Wilfulness may have many forms without a definite connection with negative emotions.

Question. It seems to me that if you give up self-will you get what you desire; that by giving up the desire, you get the desired result.

Ouspensky. That is not self-will. Self-will does not include everything you want. If you are hungry and want to eat, that is not self-will. Self-will means preferring to act by yourself and, in our case, not taking into consideration the work and the principles of the work. We speak of principles of the work and self-will. We can do things in our own way or not. If my self-will is to swear, for instance, and I give it up because it is against the principles of the work, where are the desired results you speak of?

As I said earlier, self-will is always connected with self-opinions, a man always thinks he knows something. Then he comes to a school and realizes that he knows nothing. That is why preparation is necessary for school. One is usually full of self-opinions and self-will. Self-will is like a child saying, 'I know it myself; I will do it myself'. Self-will has many features. One is told not to do something and at once one wants to do it; one is told that something is wrong, and at once one says, 'No, I know better'. A man who comes to a school must be ready to accept the teaching and the discipline of the school; he must be free to accept it, or else he will get nothing. He cannot acquire will unless he gives up self-will; just as he cannot acquire knowledge unless he gives up self-opinions.

Question. Must one break self-will oneself, or have it broken?

Ouspensky. One must do it oneself, and one must have broken it sufficiently to be in a school. One must be sufficiently free from it to accept things without a fight.

One cannot keep all the old views and opinions and acquire new ones. One must be sufficiently free to give up the old, at least for a time. One must be able to understand the necessity of discipline. Will cannot be created until one accepts a certain discipline.

Ouspensky. Suppose a man is made conscious by someone else; he will become an instrument in the hands of others. One's own efforts are necessary because otherwise even if a man is made conscious, he will not be able to use his consciousness. It is in the very nature of things that consciousness and will cannot be given. One must buy everything; nothing is given free. The most difficult thing is to learn how to pay. One gets exactly as much as one pays for, but if this could be explained in a few words there would be no need to go to school.

If you understand what development means, you will see that man can only develop by his own efforts. Will cannot develop mechanically; consciousness cannot develop unconsciously, it cannot grow out of nothing; one has to pay for everything. This brings us again to schools and the question of why one must be prepared for a school. One must realize one's position and one must be prepared to pay. The more one is prepared to pay, the more one acquires. Nothing can be given. The same thing applies to compassion. If one has something and wants to give it, one cannot. The nature of the thing one wants to give is such that people *must* pay for it. One cannot make them take it; they must want it very much and be prepared to pay for it. There is no other way. Only then can it become their own; otherwise it is lost.

Payment is something quite different from giving money or anything like that. Payment is a principle. Giving money and service is a question of possibility. Unfortunately, there is only the one word 'payment' so it has to be used in different senses. Money payment depends partly on understanding, partly on possibility. The other payment is the more important matter and it must be understood that it is absolutely necessary.

Question. I find that I work for immediate results, not for waking up. Is this a wrong aim?

Ouspensky. There is no question of right and wrong here; there is only the question of knowing your aim. Aim must always be in the present and refer to the future.

Question. Trying to define my aim has made me see that I do not know what it is and that I must find out before I can get further.

Ouspensky. I am afraid you only think about it in an abstract way. Just imagine yourself going to a big shop with many different departments. You must know what you want to buy. How can you get something if you do not know what you want? This is the way to approach the problem. The first question is: *What* do you want? Once you know this, then the next question will be: Is it worth paying for and have you enough money? But the first question is: 'What?'

Payment is a most important principle in the work and it must be understood that it is absolutely necessary. Without payment you can get nothing; and you can only get as much as you pay for — no more.

The question was put in Petersburg: 'If one pays more and more and more, so much, can one get something?' That means sacrifice. But there must not be too much self-will, even about a sacrifice.

Question. In our present state, can we judge what is a moral action?

Ouspensky. It is very easy to make mistakes but, at the same time, we can. We are just beginning. The greater our control, the greater our consciousness; and consciousness in that sense includes will. In our ordinary state, without control, we cannot speak except about conventional morality, but when we have some control we become more responsible. The less consciousness we have, the more our actions may be contrary to morality. In any case, the first necessity for moral action is that it must be conscious.

4

Negative Emotions

*

A Synthesis of some of the Sayings
and Writings of P. D. Ouspensky on
the subject of Negative Emotions

Foreword

Our starting point in this synthesis is that, ordinarily in life, nearly everything that we *feel* is imaginary and that even if it is not immediately unpleasant, it is liable to become so at any moment. The aim of the synthesis is to show that there are methods of reducing many of these imaginary and negative emotions quickly; possibilities of eliminating most of them gradually, and remote possibilities of replacing our imaginary and negative emotions with real and positive emotions.

The synthesis has been made from unpublished sayings and writings of P. D. Ouspensky, with the exception of a few descriptions of terms which have been taken from the privately printed edition of his *Psychological Lectures*, 1934–40. Whenever possible, and that is nearly always, Ouspensky's actual words have been used. In making the changes necessary to present the material in an unbroken form, care has been taken not to distort Ouspensky's meaning or add any sort of embroidery.

Summary of Contents

What is meant by 'negative emotions' 118.   Necessary to resist negative emotions 118.   Uselessness of negative emotions 118. Negative emotions cannot be controlled 118.   Negative emotions are artificial and imaginary 119.   We make excuses for our negative emotions 119.   Incompleteness of man's being 120.   Man is actually a machine 120.   The four degrees of consciousness 120. The chief functions in man 121.   Observation of functions; aim and valuation 121.   Self-remembering as means of struggling with negative emotions 122.   All negative emotions bad and a sign of weakness 123.   Negative emotions can be destroyed with benefit 123.   Causes of negative emotions are in us, not in external circumstances 123.   Capacity for feeling negative emotion depends on our own state 123.   Suffering in itself not a negative emotion 124.   Need to isolate oneself from negative emotions of other people 124.   Most negative emotions disappear if not justified 124. Struggle first with imagination and identification 125. Negative imagination must be stopped completely 125.   Struggle with expression of negative emotions different from struggle with emotions themselves 126.   Struggle with expression must come first 126.   Classifying negative emotions 126.   Preparation through right thinking 127.   Example of man who irritates you 127. Three categories of negative emotions 128.   Study of man as he may become spoilt by negative emotions 129.   Importance of right attitude 129.   Right thinking 130.   Learning to do what is possible 130.   Power of thought as method of struggling with negative emotions 130.   Thinking differently; longer thoughts 131. Habitual associations and new points of view 131.   Flashes of understanding 131.   Perceptions dependent upon degree of consciousnesᵉ 132.   Right attitude as a weapon against negative emotions 132.   Necessity for both positive and negative attitudes according to circumstances 132.   Lack of understanding due to wrong attitude 132.   Negative attitude necessary towards many things in life but positive attitude towards this work essential 133. Attitude independent of emotion 133.   Attitude can be changed 134.   Valuation 134.

1

The term 'negative emotions' means all emotions of violence or depression: self-pity, anger, suspicion, fear, annoyance, boredom, mistrust, jealousy and so on. Ordinarily, one accepts this expression of negative emotions as quite natural and even necessary. Very often people call it 'sincerity'. Of course it has nothing to do with sincerity; it is simply a sign of weakness in man, a sign of bad temper and of incapacity to keep his grievances to himself. Man realizes this when he tries to oppose it, and from this he learns another lesson. He realizes that in relation to mechanical manifestations it is not enough to observe them, it is necessary to resist them, because without resisting them one cannot observe them. They happen so quickly, so habitually and so imperceptibly that one cannot notice them if one does not make sufficient efforts to create obstacles for them.

These negative emotions are a terrible phenomenon. They occupy an enormous place in our life. Of many people it is possible to say that all their lives are regulated and controlled, and in the end ruined by negative emotions. At the same time, negative emotions do not play any useful part at all in our lives. They do not help our orientation, they do not give us any knowledge, they do not guide us in any sensible manner. On the contrary, they spoil all our pleasures, they make life a burden to us and they very effectively prevent our possible development because there is nothing more mechanical in our life than negative emotions.

Negative emotions can never come under our control. People who think they can control their negative emotions and manifest them when they want to, simply deceive themselves. Negative emotions depend on identification;[1] if identification is destroyed in some particular case, they disappear. The strangest and most fantastic fact about negative emotions is that people actually worship them. The most difficult thing for an ordinary mechanical man to realize is that his own and other people's negative emotions have no value whatever and do not contain anything noble, anything beautiful or anything strong. In reality negative emotions contain nothing but weakness and very often the beginning of hysteria, insanity or crime. The only good thing about them is that, being quite useless and artificially created by imagination and identification, they can be destroyed without any loss — and this is the only chance of escape that man has.

In reality, we have much more power over negative emotions than we think, particularly when we already know how dangerous they are and how urgent is the need to struggle with them. But we find too many excuses for them, and swim in the seas of self-pity or selfishness, as the case may be, finding fault with everything except ourselves.

1 'Identifying' or 'identification' is a curious state in which man passes about half of his life, the other half being passed in complete sleep. He identifies with everything: with what he says, what he feels, what he believes, what he does not believe, what he wishes, what he does not wish, what attracts him, what repels him. Everything becomes *him*, or it is better to say *he* becomes *it*. He becomes all that he likes and all that he dislikes. This means that in the state of identification man is incapable of separating himself from the object of his identification. It is difficult to find the smallest thing with which man is unable to identify. At the same time, in a state of identification man has even less control over his mechanical reactions than at any other time.

Identification, its meaning, causes and results, is extremely well described in *Writings from The Philokalia*, trs. by E. Kadloubovsky and G. E. Palmer, London, 1951, p. 338, paras 34-6.

2

Before saying anything further about negative emotions, it is necessary to recapitulate very briefly the fundamental idea upon which our study of man is based. Man as we know him is not a completed being; nature develops him only up to a certain point and then leaves him either to develop further by his own efforts and devices, or to live and die such as he was born. Man ascribes to himself many powers, faculties and properties which he does not possess, and which he will never possess unless he can develop into a completed being. Man does not realize that he is actually a machine, with no independent movements, which is brought into motion by external influences. The most important of the qualities which man ascribes to himself, but does not possess, is consciousness. By consciousness we mean a particular kind of awareness in man, awareness of himself, awareness of who he is, what he feels or thinks, or where he is at the moment. You must remember that man is not equally conscious all the time and that, according to the way in which we study man, we consider that he has the possibility of four states of consciousness. They are: *sleep, waking-state* or *relative consciousness, third state of consciousness* or *self-consciousness,* and *fourth state of consciousness* or *objective consciousness,* but in ordinary life man knows nothing of objective consciousness and no experiments in this direction are possible. In fact man actually lives only in two states: one part of his life passes in sleep, and the other part in what is called waking-state, though in reality it differs very little from sleep. When we speak of consciousness, therefore, we refer to a state of greater consciousness than our ordinary waking state. We have no control over this state but we have a certain control over the way in which we think about it and we can construct our thinking in such a way as to bring consciousness. By giving to our thoughts a direction which they would have in a moment of consciousness we can induce consciousness. This practice we call *self-remembering*.[2]

Further, in relation to our study of man we spoke of the necessity for us to understand the four chief functions of the human machine — thinking, feeling, moving, instinctive — and to try to observe the differences in quality of their manifestation in each of the three states of consciousness. All four functions can manifest themselves in sleep, but their manifestations are desultory and unreliable; they cannot be used in any way, they just go by themselves. In the state of relative consciousness or waking-state, they can, to a certain extent, serve for our orientation. Their results can be compared, verified, straightened out, and although they may create many illusions, still in our ordinary state we have nothing else and must make of them what we can. If we knew the quantity of wrong observations, wrong theories, wrong deductions and conclusions made in this state, we should cease to believe ourselves altogether. But men do not realize how deceptive their observations and their theories can be, and they continue to believe in them. It is this that keeps man from observing the rare moments when their functions manifest themselves in connection with glimpses of the third state of consciousness or self-consciousness.

Observing of functions is long work. It is necessary to find many examples of each. In studying, we begin to see that we cannot study everything on the same level, that we cannot observe ourselves impartially. Unavoidably we see that some functions are right and others undesirable from

2 Self-remembering is described in *In Search of the Miraculous* by P. D. Ouspensky, New York, 1949, pp. 117 f.

the point of view of our aim. And we must have an aim, otherwise no study can have any result. If we realize that we are asleep, the aim is to awaken; if we realize that we are machines, the aim is to cease to be machines. If we want to be more conscious, we must study what prevents us from remembering ourselves. So we have to introduce a certain valuation of functions from the point of view of whether they are useful or harmful for self-remembering.

If you make a serious effort to observe functions for yourself, you will realize one thing. You will realize that ordinarily, whatever you do, whatever you think, whatever you feel, you do not remember yourself. At the same time you will find that, if you make sufficient efforts for a sufficiently long time, you can increase your capacity for self-remembering. You will begin to remember yourself more often, and more deeply; you will begin to remember yourself in connection with more ideas, such as the idea of consciousness, the idea of work, and the idea of self-study.

The question is: how are we to remember ourselves, how are we to make ourselves more aware?

If you think seriously about negative emotions, you will find that they are the chief factors which prevent us from remembering ourselves. So the one thing cannot go without the other. You cannot struggle with negative emotions without remembering yourself more, and you cannot remember yourself more without struggling with negative emotions.

3

In order to begin to struggle with negative emotions it is first of all necessary to realize that there is not a single useful negative emotion. Negative emotions are all equally bad and all a sign of weakness. Next we have to realize that we *can* struggle with them, that they can be conquered and destroyed because there is no real centre for them. If there were a real centre for them, we should have no chance; we should remain for ever in the power of negative emotions. Luckily for us they exist in an artificial centre which can be destroyed and lost, and we shall feel much better if it is. Even the realization that this is possible is very much; but we have so many convictions, prejudices and even principles about it, that it is difficult to get rid of the idea that negative emotions are necessary and obligatory. As long as we think that they are necessary, unavoidable, and even useful for self-expression or many other things, we can do nothing. It is necessary to have a certain mental struggle to realize that negative emotions are quite useless, that they have no useful function in our lives and yet, at the same time, that all life is based on them. That is what nobody realizes.

One of the strongest illusions is to think that negative emotions are produced by circumstances, and we speak of being angry 'for some perfectly just reason', but all negative emotions are in us, *inside us*. Before we can begin to struggle with them, we must realize that there are no just reasons for being angry. We think — and we like to think — that our negative emotions are produced either by the fault of other people or by the fault of circumstances. This is an illusion. My anger is not in the reason, it is in me. Your anger is not in the reason, it is in you. The causes of negative emotions are not in external reasons, they are in ourselves. There is absolutely not a single unavoidable reason whereby somebody else's action or certain circumstances should produce negative emotion in me. It is only my weakness.

If you observe yourself, you will see that although the

causes outside remain the same, they sometimes produce negative emotion in you and sometimes not. The reason for this is that the real cause of the negative emotion is in you and the external event is only the apparent cause. If you are in a good state, if you are remembering yourself, if you are not identifying, then — relatively speaking and barring catastrophes — nothing that happens outside can produce negative emotion in you. If you are in a bad state, identified, immersed in imagination or something like that, then everything just a little unpleasant will produce violent emotion in you.

In an attempt to show that negative emotions are produced by an outside cause, questions are sometimes asked about such things as grief at the death of a friend and other kinds of suffering. Suffering, in itself, is not negative emotion. It can produce negative emotion only if you identify with it. Suffering can be real; negative emotion is not real. After all, suffering occupies a very small part of life but negative emotions occupy a big part — they occupy the whole of life. And why? Because we justify them. We think that they are produced by some external cause. Certainly, people who are full of negative emotions and identification are likely to produce similar reactions in other people, but one must learn to isolate oneself in such cases by means of self-remembering and not identifying, realizing at the same time that isolation does not mean indifference. When we know that negative emotions cannot be produced by external causes, most of them disappear. But the first condition is that we must realize fully that they *cannot* be produced by external causes if we do not wish to have them. They are generally there because we permit them, explaining their presence as being due to external causes, so that we do not struggle with them. Negative emotions cannot exist without imagination. Simply suffering pain is not a negative emotion, but when imagination and identification enter, then it becomes negative emotion. Emotional pain, like physical pain, is not negative emotion by itself, but when we begin to make all kinds of embroidery on it, it becomes emotion.

4

Later we may come to methods for struggling with emotions themselves, because there are many and very definite methods, different for different emotions, but first you must struggle with identification and imagination. People ascribe to the word imagination a quite artificial and quite undeserved meaning in the sense of creative or selective faculty. Imagination is a destructive faculty which cannot be controlled. We start to imagine something in order to please ourselves and very soon we begin to believe it or at least some of it. Imagination generally consists in ascribing to oneself some knowledge, some power, some quality which one does not possess. This is dangerous imagination, whereas just letting things come into the mind or day-dreaming may be harmless and even pleasant as long as it is free from identification. This struggle with identification and imagination is sufficient to destroy many of the usual negative emotions — in any case, to make them much lighter. You must start with this because it is only possible to begin using stronger methods against negative emotions when you can struggle with identification to a certain extent, and when you have already stopped negative imagination. That must be stopped completely. It is useless to study further methods until that is done. If you try to eliminate imagination, there is no danger of eliminating real feeling; if it is real it cannot be eliminated. Negative imagination you *can* stop; and even the study of identification will already diminish it, but the real struggle with negative emotions themselves begins later. It is based on right understanding, first of all, of how they are created, what is behind them, how useless they are and how much you lose because of the pleasure you take in having negative emotions. When you realize how much you lose, perhaps you will have enough energy to do something about it.

5

It is necessary for you to understand that the stopping of the *expression* of negative emotions and the struggle with negative emotions themselves are two quite different practices. Trying to stop the expression comes first. You can do nothing about negative emotions themselves until you have learned to stop the expression of them. When you have acquired a certain control over the expression of negative emotion, you can begin to study negative emotions in themselves. You can make an effort to classify your negative emotions. You can find which negative emotions you have chiefly; why they come, what brings them, and so on. You must understand that your only control over emotions is through your mind, but the control does not come immediately. If you think rightly for six months, then negative emotions will be affected because they are based on wrong thinking. If you begin to think rightly today, negative emotions will not be changed tomorrow; but negative emotions may be changed in six months' time, if you start to think rightly now. The ground has to be prepared beforehand. If you can learn to create a right attitude towards your irritability, bad temper, suspicion or whatever unpleasant emotion you experience most frequently, then — after some time — that attitude will help you to stop the negative emotion at the beginning. Once it has been allowed to start you cannot stop it. Once you begin to express it, you are in its power. The struggle must begin in your mind, and you must find your way of thinking on a definite subject. You cannot control your temper when it has already begun to appear. It is already too late; it has already jumped out. You can control such things as manifestations of temper, for instance, only in one way. Suppose you have to meet a certain man, and suppose he irritates you. Whenever you meet him your temper is liable to show itself. You do not like that but how can you stop it? You must begin with the study of your thinking. What do you *think* about this man — not what do you *feel* when you are irritated, but what do you think about him at quiet moments? You may find that in your mind you argue with him; you prove to him that he is wrong; you tell him all his mistakes; you find that, generally, he behaves wrongly towards you. This is where you are wrong. You must learn to think rightly; you must find the way to think rightly. Then, if you do, it will happen like this: although emotion is much quicker than thought, emotion is a temporary thing, but thought can be made continuous; so whenever emotion jumps out, it hits against this continuous thought and cannot go on and manifest itself. So you can struggle with the expression of negative emotions, as in this example, only by creating continuous right thinking. We shall return presently to the question of what is meant by right thinking and right attitude as weapons against negative emotions.

6

It is necessary to repeat that first of all you *must* understand how wrong negative emotions are, how useless they
are, and then you must understand that they cannot exist
without identification. It will take you a long time to
realize this, but when you have done so, you must try to
divide your negative emotions into three categories. First,
the more or less ordinary everyday negative emotions
which happen often, and are always connected with
identification. Certainly, you must observe them and you
must already have a certain control over the expression of
them. Then you must start dealing with them by trying
not to identify, by avoiding identification as often as you
can, not only in relation to these emotions but in relation
to everything. If you create in yourself the capacity of not
identifying, that will affect these emotions and you will
notice how they begin to disappear.

The second category do not appear every day. They are
the more difficult, more complicated emotions depending
on some mental process — suspicion, hurt feelings and
many things like that. They are more difficult to conquer.
You can deal with them by creating a right mental
attitude, by thinking — not at the time when you are in
the negative emotion, but in between, when you are quiet.
Try to find the right attitude, the right point of view, and
make it permanent. If you create right thinking, that will
take all power from these negative emotions.

Then there is a third category, much more intense,
much more difficult, and very rare. Against them you can
do nothing. These two methods — struggle with identification and creating right attitudes — do not help. When
such emotions come you can do only one thing: you must
try to remember yourself; to remember yourself with the

help of the emotion. That will change them after some time. But for this you have to be prepared; it is quite a special thing.

7

We study ourselves not from the point of view of what we are but of what we may become, so that when we have studied certain things sufficiently, we work to change them. Sufficiently serious study, in itself, produces some change, but all the results of this change may be spoiled by certain negative emotions. If you start this work to change yourself without conquering negative emotions, one side of you will work and another side will spoil your work, so that after a time, you may find yourself in a worse state than before. It has already happened several times to people who wished to keep their negative emotions that continuation of this work became impossible for them. There were moments when they realized the danger of their negative emotions but they failed to make sufficient efforts during those moments and the negative emotions became stronger. It has been explained already that a right attitude towards negative emotions destroys most of them. If we are to avoid spoiling the results of our work, it is important that we learn to cultivate this attitude from the beginning.

A right attitude towards a subject is the result of right thinking about that definite subject. For instance, many people live only on objections; they only think themselves clever when they find an objection to something. When they do not find any objection, they do not feel themselves to be working or thinking or anything. Again, nearly all our personal negative emotions are based upon accusation, and upon the assumption that somebody else is guilty. If, by persistent thinking, we realize that nobody can be guilty in relation to us and that we are the cause of everything that happens to us, our attitude towards those emotions of accusation will begin to change. Eventually this right thinking, this creation of a right attitude or point of view may become a permanent process, and then negative emotions will only appear occasionally. Exactly by being permanent this process of right thinking has power over negative emotions; it checks them right at the beginning.

We can learn to refuse some points of view and to accept other points of view. From one point of view we are so mechanical and we can do nothing, while from another point of view there are in us — perhaps not many but several — things which we can begin to do. We have certain possibilities in us which we do not use. It is true that you cannot *do* anything, in the sense that you cannot change what you *feel* at any given moment, but you can make yourself *think* about a subject at a given moment. This is the beginning. You must know what is possible and begin from that, because the possibility to do something instead of letting something happen will increase quickly. You can make yourself think about a subject in a certain way, and — when it is necessary — you can make yourself not think.

You do not realize what enormous power lies in thinking. That is not meant as a philosophical explanation of power. The power lies in the fact that, if you always think rightly about certain things, you can make that thought permanent and it will grow into a permanent attitude. If you find in yourself an inclination to a wrong emotional manifestation of some kind, you can do nothing about it just at that moment because you have educated in yourself the capacity for this kind of reaction by wrong thinking; but after some time of right thinking, you may educate in yourself the capacity for a different reaction. Only, this method *has to be understood* and this understanding *must be quite deep.* You can apply this method to many different things. This is really the one thing you can do. You can do nothing else. There is no direct way to struggle with negative manifestations because you cannot catch them; and there is no way to prevent them except by being prepared beforehand for them. A passing realization that they are wrong will not help; it must be very deep, otherwise you will again have an equally difficult process to prepare the ground for another manifestation. You have to realize how much you lose by these spontaneous manifestations of a negative character. They make so many desirable things impossible, and you lose exactly what you want to get.

8

In order to have a right attitude about things, we must learn to think differently, and to have *longer thoughts.* Each of our thoughts is too short. Until you have experience from your own observation of the difference between long and short thoughts, this idea will mean nothing to you.

As long as we allow our thinking to depend entirely upon habitual association, it will not improve; but by introducing new points of view, we can create new associations. For instance, we are accustomed to think in absolutes — all or nothing — but it is necessary to understand that anything new comes at first in flashes. It comes, then it disappears. Only after a certain time these flashes become longer and then still longer, so that you can see and notice them. Nothing comes at once in a complete form. Everything that can be acquired comes, then disappears, comes again, again disappears. After a long time it comes and stays a little, so that you are able to give a name to it, to notice it. I do not want to give an example because it would lead to imagination. All I will say is that, for instance, by certain efforts of self-remembering one could see certain things that one cannot see now. Our eyes are not as limited as we think. There are many things that they can see but do not notice. We cannot perceive differently until we think differently. We have control only over thoughts; we have no control over perception. Perception does not depend upon our desire or decision, it depends particularly on our state of consciousness, on our being more awake. If one awakens for a sufficient time, say for one hour, one can see many things that one does not see now.

9

The question of using a right attitude as a weapon against negative emotions requires understanding; it refers to our attitude to the emotions themselves, because we may have a right or a wrong attitude to our negativeness. It is different in different cases and there can be no generalization. Now we must consider the attitudes in themselves and realize that a positive attitude is right in some cases, and that a negative attitude is right in other cases. A positive attitude belongs to the part of our intellect which says 'Yes' and a negative attitude to the part which says 'No'. There can also be different attitudes but these are the two most important. Lack of understanding about some subject or problem may be caused simply by having a wrong attitude towards it. There are people who have a negative attitude towards everything and anything, and there are others who try to cultivate a positive attitude about things towards which they should have a negative attitude. Using the words 'positive' and 'negative' in the ordinary sense of approval or disapproval, we can say that in order to understand certain things we must have negative attitudes whereas other things can be understood positively. Too much of an indiscriminately positive attitude can spoil things in the same way as a persistently negative attitude towards everything can spoil things, but sometimes a negative attitude is useful because there are many things in life which can only be understood through having a sufficiently good negative attitude towards them. Certainly, identification with a negative attitude would cause negative emotion, but this can be avoided, and very often identifying is the result of a wrong attitude. Paradoxical as it may seem, we have many negative emotions because we do not have a sufficiently negative attitude towards negative emotions. On the other hand, the moment you have a negative attitude towards any of the things connected with this work of development, you will cease to understand it.

We must understand that we have no control, that we are machines, that everything happens to us. Simply to speak about it does not change these facts. To cease to be mechanical something else is needed. A change of attitude is necessary. Attitude can be independent of emotion, and to a certain extent it can be under our control. For instance, we have some control over our attitudes towards knowledge, towards friends, towards this work and towards self-study. Attitude is really a point of view, and if a point of view is right, there is one effect; if it is wrong, another effect. It is necessary to understand that we cannot do things, but we can change our attitudes.

A right attitude may be developed gradually through the study of oneself and the study of life, in accordance with the special way in which we study it. This study does not depend only on knowledge but upon a different way of thinking. Different thinking can only come from different attitudes and from an understanding of the relative values of things. Change of attitude does not bring about change of a man's being by itself. Valuation is necessary.

5

Notes on Work

Contents

Notes on Decision to Work   137
Notes on Work on Oneself   140
What is School?   149

Notes on Decision to Work

Think very seriously before you decide to work on yourself with the idea of changing yourself, i.e. to work with the definite aim of becoming conscious and of developing connection with higher centres. This work admits of no compromise and it requires a great amount of self-discipline and readiness to obey all rules and particularly, direct instructions.

Think very seriously: are you really ready and willing to obey, and do you fully understand the necessity for it? There is no going back. If you agree and then go back, you will lose everything that you have acquired up to that time, and you will lose more really, because all that you acquired will turn into something wrong in you. There is no remedy against this.

Understanding of the necessity for obeying rules and direct instructions must be based on the realization of your mechanicalness and your helplessness. If this realization is not strong enough, you had better wait and occupy yourself with ordinary work; study of the system, work in groups, etc. If you do this work sincerely and remember all rules, it will bring you to the realization of your state and your needs. But you must not delay too long. If you want to come to real work you must hurry. You must understand that the opportunity that exists today may not come your way again. You may lose all your chances by hesitating and waiting too long.

If you decide to work and accept all that comes in the work, you must learn to think quickly. If you are offered a task you must answer *at once* that you accept it. If you hesitate or take time to answer, the offer of the task will be withdrawn and it will not be repeated. You may be given time before actually doing what you were told to do, but you must accept the task at once. An attempt to talk things over, an ironical, suspicious or negative attitude, fear, or lack of confidence, these will make the task impossible at once. If you feel hesitation about the task offered to you, think about your mechanicalness, think about your negativeness, about your self-will — but think quickly. You can do nothing against your weak sides by yourself. The tasks offered to you have the aim of helping you. If you hesitate or refuse them, you refuse help. This must be quite clear in your mind.

The realization of your helplessness and your deep sleep must be permanent in you. You can strengthen it by constantly reminding yourself of your nothingness, of your meanness, of your weakness of all possible sorts. You have absolutely nothing to be proud of. You have nothing to base your judgement on. You can see, if you are sincere with yourself, all the blunders and all the mistakes which you made when you tried to act by yourself. You cannot think rightly. You cannot feel rightly. You need constant help, and you can have it. But you must pay for it — at least, by not arguing.

You have to do gigantic work if you want to become different. How can you ever hope to get anything if you hesitate and argue on the first steps, or do not even realize the necessity for help, or become suspicious and negative?

If you want to work seriously you have to conquer many things in yourself. You cannot carry with yourself your prejudices, your fixed opinions, your personal identifications or animosities.

But at the same time try to understand that personal is not always wrong. Personal can even help in the work but personal can be very dangerous too, if it is not cleared by the struggle with identification and by the realization of your mechanicalness and your weakness.

Try to understand the necessity for deliberate suffering and conscious effort. These are the only two things that can change you and bring you to your aim.

Deliberate suffering does not mean necessary suffering inflicted on you by yourself. It means attitude towards suffering. Suffering may come as a result of your feelings, thoughts and actions connected with your task; it may come by itself as a result of your own faults or as a result of other people's actions, attitudes or feelings. But what is important is your attitude towards it. It becomes deliberate if you do not rebel against it, if you do not try to avoid it, if you do not accuse anybody, if you accept it as a necessary part of your work at the moment, and as a means for attaining your aim.

Conscious effort is the effort based on understanding; understanding of its necessity first of all, and understanding of causes which make it necessary. The chief cause for conscious effort is your need for breaking the walls of mechanicalness, of self-will and of lack of self-remembering which constitute your being at present.

In order to understand better the necessity for accepting tasks given to you without hesitation, the necessity for deliberate suffering and conscious effort, think about ideas which brought you to the work, think about the first realization of your mechanicalness and the first realization that you know nothing. In the beginning you realized this and you came for help, but now you doubt whether you must really do as you are told. And you try to find ways to evade it, to stand on your own judgement and on your own understanding. You understood clearly once, that your judgement and your understanding are false and weak, but now you try to keep them again. You do not want to give them up. Well, you can keep them, but you must understand that with them you will keep all that is

false and weak in yourself. There are no half measures.
You must decide. Do you want to work or not?

Notes on Work on Oneself

Try to remember and keep in your mind constantly all the
lines on which you have to work. You have to work on
mind, on consciousness, on emotions and on will. Try to
understand that each line of work needs special attention,
special methods and special understanding. After some
time all four will begin to help one another and later they
will merge into one, but in the beginning the four lines
must go separately.

Try to understand the work on *mind*. To do this work
you must constantly revise all ideas of the system referring
to man and the universe, and particularly those referring to
psychology, the study of emotions, many 'I's, the division
of man, false personality, permanent 'I', esotericism,
schools and methods of school work. Keep your mind on
these ideas or at least return to them as often as possible.
Your mind must never be idle. At every possible moment
you must reflect on one or another idea, on one or another
aspect of the system and methods.

Try to understand the necessity for introducing the
methods and principles of the work in your *personal life*
and first of all the necessity for right thinking on all
personal questions and their possible relation to your
work. Without this, you will never reach unity. You
cannot allow one part of yourself to think wrongly and
hope that another part will think rightly.

Understanding of principles, rules and methods of
school work is one of the most important parts of the
work on mind. Mind must be trained not to hesitate in its

choice between right and wrong, must understand perfectly right relations to me, to other people in the work and to the people outside.

Mind must understand that in the very beginning of serious work on oneself one gives up one's freedom. Certainly it is an illusionary freedom, but when one puts oneself under the laws of the work, one is naturally under more laws than someone outside the work.

Try to understand the meaning of *silence* in the work, the meaning of *sincerity* and the meaning of *truth*.

One can never expect to get anything from the work if one cannot keep silence when it is not necessary to speak for the sake of the work. People generally talk too much, talk for their own gratification, from self-pride, from vanity, from desire to live again through pleasant or painful experiences; they talk because they cannot resist identification with talking or because they do not realize that they should not talk in this particular way or on this particular subject. Very often the special attraction of talking, for them, is in the fact that they know that they should not talk.

I do not even mean talking to people outside the work. That must have been dealt with long before any possibility of serious work on oneself arises.

What I mean is that one must be very guarded even in speaking to one's friends in the work, unless one is told by me to speak.

Also, one cannot expect anything if one cannot be sincere with oneself and with me. With other people in the work one can have a mutual arrangement regarding sincerity about everything or about particular subjects, but this can only be done with my approval and with my complete knowledge of what is said.

Further, one cannot expect to get anything from the

work if one is afraid or reluctant to speak the truth to me even without being told to do so.

You must understand that nobody who wishes to remain in the work can ask another person in the work to keep something secret from me, and nobody can give the promise to keep anything secret. This is a very important point.

One must always be ready to tell me anything about oneself and anything one may learn about another person. And one must do so by oneself without being reminded, and do it with full understanding that this is an essential part of the work.

You must understand that you cannot accept part of the rules and reject or forget another part. You must understand the importance of discipline in the work.

You must understand the meaning of the words: *sacrifice your suffering*, and the right moments, right methods and the aim and possible results of such sacrifice.

You must understand the necessity for being careful when saying 'I'. You can say 'I' when speaking about yourself only when you are sure that you speak about work or ideas or rules and principles of the work, or in accordance with all rules and principles. In all other cases you must try to understand which part of you is speaking or thinking, and name it accordingly. This idea must not be exaggerated. You can say without harm: I am going to buy some cigarettes. But you cannot say: I dislike this man. You must find which part of you dislikes him and why, and not ascribe this dislike to all of you.

You must clearly understand the necessity of self-observation for self study. You must understand the difference between functions and consciousness. Thinking of functions, you must always be able to distinguish the intellectual, emotional, moving and instinctive functions;

positive and negative parts of centres in the intellectual and instinctive centres; moving, emotional and intellectual parts in all centres. You must study attention and understand how, by the study of attention, you can distinguish parts of centres.

In relation to the study of *consciousness* you must remember what you know about sleep and waking state, the different levels in waking state, and the connection of higher centres with higher states of consciousness. You must remember that your aim is to produce higher states of consciousness in yourself and to establish connection with higher centres. You must understand that higher centres have many unknown functions which cannot be described in ordinary language. They have much more power, and a deeper penetration into the laws of nature. You must remember that many problems insoluble for our ordinary mind can become soluble for higher centres. And you must always return to the idea of permanent 'I' and realize how far you are from it and how many efforts and sacrifices are necessary in order to reach it.

In the work on *consciousness* you must understand first of all, that this work is entirely practical. Theoretical study will not help. Second, you must understand that the work on consciousness can give results only when it becomes permanent or as near to permanent as possible. Spasmodic, accidental, interrupted work cannot give results. So try to find how you can make your work on consciousness continuous. Your mind must guide you in the beginning, constantly reminding you of the necessity for remembering yourself, and helping you to catch the moments of not remembering.

But realize that mind can only *prepare* you for this work and only guide you for a certain distance. You can go further in the work on consciousness only with the help of will and emotions.

Remember also, that consciousness can be measured by the length of periods of consciousness and by the frequency of the appearance of these periods.

Efforts to create consciousness in oneself feel almost hopeless in the beginning. But very soon they will begin to give results. You will notice these results by observing moments of consciousness appearing by themselves without any effort on your part. In reality, they are the results of previous efforts.

The practice of stopping thoughts helps self-remembering very much. Struggle with imagination and with mechanical talk with oneself or with people is necessary from the very beginning. But one will get still stronger help for self-remembering from sacrificing one's suffering. Only this can make the work on consciousness real and serious. Before this, all is only preparation for it.

The work on *emotions* as the work on consciousness must be practical from the beginning. It begins with the struggle against the expression of negative emotions. When a certain control is acquired and when you fully understand all evil sides of negative emotions in your own life and in life in general, you must make a plan for your personal work on identification, imagination and lying in those particular forms which they take in you.

In this work you must not be afraid to hurt yourself. Understand that only by hurting yourself can you get what you want. You can do this by observing rules. For instance, by saying something about yourself or about other people that you do not want to say, but when you are told to do so. Also, you can produce a very emotional state in yourself by preparing yourself to speak in this way, that is, by imagining yourself being told to speak the truth on the most difficult and intimate subjects which you think are quite hidden or disguised.

Realize also, that there are many other kinds of suffering through which you will pass before you attain your aim. Try to understand that suffering is *the only active principle in us* which can be converted into higher feeling — which is also higher thought and higher understanding.

Do not be afraid of thinking of your emotions and finding contradictions in them, even if it hurts you. Only by comparing different emotions referring to the same subject can you find buffers in yourself and eventually destroy them if you work hard enough and are not afraid of hurting yourself.

Remember that this will lead you to the awakening of conscience, which is the simultaneous feeling of all contradictory emotions; and remember that the awakening of conscience is a necessary step for transferring yourself to the higher level of consciousness.

Practice removing identification and imagination from negative emotions without destroying them. You may get quite unexpected and very interesting results.

Learn to transform emotions into mental attitudes and to transfer them to the mind. Many emotions which are quite useless and even harmful in emotional centre, because they cannot exist there without identification and imagination, become quite useful as mental attitudes and help self-observation, observation of other people and general understanding.

Try to go through all your emotions during all the time you have been connected with the system, emotions referring to the system itself, to me, to yourself and to other people in the work.

Try to be sincere with yourself. See how you have always tried to profit by your being in the work; for instance, by using the particular intimacy that establishes itself between people in the work, owing to common psychological study and the disappearance of many buffers, for making friends in the ordinary mechanical and sentimental way, having love affairs, etc. See what use you have made of your connection with the work. See how you were often selfish and calculating, how little you gave to the work and how much you took from it. See how much considering was in your attitudes, how many demands and how much resentment, particularly when people tried to help you. Try to see how poor was your valuation of the work and how much you missed by it. Try to see how foolish you were to express negative opinions of people who could have helped you, many of whom have disappeared already. Try to see yourself as you really are. And do not let yourself rest, do not comfort yourself with false hopes and expectations of miracles, or with decisions to act differently tomorrow.

Think about life in general, think about masses of blind and sleeping people without any chance in the world to become anything else. Think about yourself, realize how many opportunities you had and how many you have already lost and continue to lose daily.

Think about death. You do not know how much time remains to you. And remember that if you do not become different, everything will be repeated again, all foolish blunders, all silly mistakes, all loss of time and opportunity — everything will be repeated with the exception of the *chance* you had this time, because *chance* never comes in the same form.

You will have to *look for* your chance next time. And in order to do this, you will have to remember many things, and how will you remember then if you do not remember anything now?

Try to understand the work on *will*. You begin this work by work on mind and consciousness; work on emotions strengthens will still more, and prepares you for further efforts. But real work on will begins with trying to understand self-will and finding examples of its manifest-ations in your actions. At this point comes the necessity for great sincerity with yourself and the necessity for being ready to speak to me about your manifestations of self-will. Try to understand that every decision made by yourself and for yourself which can at the same time affect your work is the manifestation of self-will.

In order to understand better the difference between will and self-will, learn to distinguish between mechanical and conscious. Self-will is always mechanical, will is always conscious. You must understand that even on an ordinary level there is a great difference between mechanical and conscious. In life the difference is connected with the difference between important and unimportant, but in life the difference between important and unimportant varies for different people and changes according to the change of circumstances. For people in schools, 'important' is always connected with the work.

If you consider yourself connected with school work or wish to be in school work but hesitate in relation to life matters and do not know which way to choose, you can always find what is more important for you by looking at the question from this point of view.

'Important' is always, in one way or in many ways, connected with the work and cannot contradict principles and methods of the work. Mechanical decisions and mechanical actions always contradict the methods of the work, and harm your work and your position in the work.

If you cannot decide yourself what is more important and which way to choose, *you must ask me*.

If you are seriously in the work and want to be in the work, you must not make any decision which may affect your life without first asking my opinion. Your own decisions in serious cases are bound to be based on self-will.

But you cannot ask my opinion or my decision when your decision is already made and you have already begun to act on the basis of it, because that means self-will in action, and in such a case it is too late to ask me. Questions as to my opinion and my decision when your decision is already made, are really manifestations of insincerity with yourself and attempts to deceive me by false pretences.

Try to realize that mechanical actions and mechanical decisions are always based on considerations outside the work (even if you persuade yourself that the result will be useful for your work), considerations of pleasure, of convenience or comfort; or they result from negative emotions or imagination.

Try to understand that if you are in the work and wish to be in the work the most mechanical manifestation is lying to me or suppressing the truth from me.

Demand for complete truth does not refer to people only beginning to work with me. They must make long preliminary work on mind and consciousness before complete truth becomes necessary and obligatory. But when they realize the necessity for personal help, and when I find that they are ready and I can help them, the principle of complete truth becomes obligatory. And it is certainly obligatory for all people who have been in the work for five years and also for some who have been in the work much less but have already formulated their aim.

Remember that your chief work must be on self-will. One begins to give up one's self-will by accepting rules, but one must be sincere about it. Later one must give up one's self-will in all serious matters and accept another person's will, in this case, mine. Only by doing this, and doing it with full understanding of the necessity for doing so, one will begin to acquire slowly one's own will. Really, the very act of giving up one's self-will is the first act and the first manifestation of real will.

The four lines of work on oneself can be designated: intellectual work — *preparation*; work on consciousness — *aim*; work on emotions — *means, energy*; work on will — *control,* and also *energy.*

What is School?

Question. What is school?
Ouspensky. School is an organization for the transmission to a certain number of prepared people of knowledge coming from higher mind.

The most essential thing in school is the knowledge which comes from higher mind. This means that schools cannot be formed arbitrarily without the participation of people who have obtained knowledge in schools. Another very important fact is the selection effected by the school, that is, the selection of students. Only people of a certain preparation and a certain level of understanding are admitted. A school cannot be open to all, it cannot even be open to many. A school is always a closed circle with the instructor in the centre.

Schools can be of very different levels depending on the preparation and the level of being of the students. The higher the level of the school the greater the demands made upon the students.

Question. Why are schools necessary?
Ouspensky. Before speaking of *why* schools are necessary

it must be realized *for whom* schools are necessary, because schools are not necessary at all for the vast majority of people. Schools are necessary to those people who already realize the inadequacy of knowledge collected by the ordinary mind and who feel that, by themselves, with their own strength they can neither resolve the problems which surround them nor find the right way. Only such people are capable of overcoming the difficulties connected with school work and only for them are schools necessary.

In order to understand *why* schools are necessary it must be realised that the knowledge which comes from men of higher mind can be transmitted only to a very limited number of people simultaneously and with the necessary observance of a whole series of definite conditions which must be well known to the instructor of the school and without which knowledge cannot be transmitted *correctly*.

The existence of these conditions and the impossibility of doing without them explains the necessity of an organization. The transmission of knowledge demands efforts both on the part of him who receives it and on the part of him who gives it. The organization facilitates these efforts or makes them possible. These conditions cannot come about by themselves. A school can only be organized according to a certain definite plan worked out and known long ago. There can be nothing arbitrary and improvised in schools. But schools can be of different type corresponding to different ways. Different ways will be spoken of later.

Question. Can it be explained in what these conditions consist?

Ouspensky. These conditions are connected with a definite property of man's nature, namely, that there are two sides of man which, in man's general development, ought to develop simultaneously and in parallel: *knowledge* and *being*. People know, or think they know, what knowledge is and to a certain extent they understand the relativity of knowledge. But they do not know what being is and they do not understand the relativity of being and the fact that knowledge depends on being. Meanwhile the development of knowledge without corresponding development of being or a development of being without a corresponding development of knowledge gives wrong results. Schools are necessary in order to avoid such one-sided development and the undesirable results connected with it. The conditions of school teaching are such that from the very first steps work progresses simultaneously along two lines, along the line of knowledge and along the line of being. From the first days at school a man begins to study mechanicalness and to struggle against mechanicalness in himself, against involuntary actions, against unnecessary talk, against imagination, against day-dreaming and against sleep. It is explained to him that his knowledge depends on his being. In making one step along the line of knowledge a man must make a step along the line of being. The principles of school work, all the demands made upon him, the rules which he must remember, all help him to study his being and to work to change it.

Question. Why is knowledge necessary?

Ouspensky. The aim of a man who realizes his state and his position becomes a change of being. This change is so difficult that it would, in fact, be impossible if knowledge was not there to help him.

Question. Can a change of being, that is, the attainment of a certain level of being, give knowledge?

Ouspensky. No, it cannot. Knowledge and being express two sides of man's nature which can develop and grow, but they require different efforts for their development.

Question. On what does understanding depend, on knowledge or on being?

Ouspensky. Neither knowledge nor being separately can give right understanding. The reason for this is that understanding is the resultant of knowledge and being. A growth of understanding is possible only with a simultaneous growth of knowledge and being. If one outgrows the other too much, understanding cannot develop in the right direction.

Question. What is meant by growth of knowledge and growth of being?

Ouspensky. The growth of knowledge means a transition from the particular to the general, from details to the whole, from the illusory to the real. Ordinary knowledge, or what is called knowledge, is always a knowledge of details without a knowledge of the whole, a knowledge of the leaves, or the veins and serrations in the leaves, without a knowledge of the tree. Real knowledge not only shows a given detail, but the place, the function and the meaning of this detail in the whole. In our ordinary knowledge there are times which bring us near to real knowledge. For instance, in the ordinary system of notation any number not only defines the power but shows the place of this power in the series of powers from zero to infinity. All real knowledge is of this nature.

Real knowledge comes from higher mind, that is, from the minds of men who have attained the fullest development possible for men. It is called *objective knowledge,* as distinct from the knowledge of ordinary men, which is called subjective knowledge. Objective knowledge is always *school* knowledge, that is, knowledge acquired in a school. A man cannot arrive at it with his own mind or get it from books.

One of the first ideas of objective knowledge is that a

knowledge of the real world is possible, but only on the condition of being able to make use of the principles of *relativity* and *scale* and then of knowing the fundamental laws of the universe, the *law of three* and the *law of seven.* The approach to the study of objective knowledge begins with the study of an objective language. The next step is the study of oneself which begins with the understanding of man's place in the universe and the study of the human machine. The knowledge of oneself is both an aim and a means.

A man who has not had school teaching, that is, a man of a subjective way of thinking, lives surrounded by illusions, first of all about himself. He thinks that he has will and the possibility of choice every moment of his life; he thinks that he can *do*; he thinks that he has individuality, that is, something permanent and unchange-able; he thinks he has an 'I' or an Ego likewise permanent and unchangeable; he considers himself a *conscious being* and supposes that he is able to arrange life on earth by following the indications of reason and logic; his usual state of consciousness, in which he lives and acts, he calls *clear consciousness* when in reality it is sleep. In this sleep he lives, writes books, invents theories, carries on wars, kills other sleeping people and dies himself without even suspecting for a moment that he can awake.

He does not realize the possibility of development or growth. He ascribes to himself that which he does not possess. But he does not know how much it is that he could acquire.

If he is a man of scientific views he does not admit the possibility of any individual evolution of man beyond the limits of ordinary intellectual development during life. Instead he acknowledges the possibility of the evolution of man *as a species* and he considers such evolution to be entirely mechanical, that is, not dependent upon anybody's will.

If he is a religious man he believes in a future life and that he is guided *for his own good* by higher powers with whom he can have intercourse by means of prayer.

If he is familiar with theosophy he believes in the law of Karma and in reincarnation; he considers that he has an astral body, a mental body and a causal body, and that through an inevitable evolution he will attain to the very highest degrees, if not on earth then on some other planet.

If he has already understood the inadequacy and the illusory nature of scientific, religious and theosophical ideas and realizes the necessity for inner change in man, he does not realize the difficulty of this, he does not realize the necessity for lengthy and systematic efforts which are impossible without a knowledge of methods and without an exact and detailed knowledge of the human machine. It seems to him that what *can* come *must* come.

But in reality nothing comes of itself. A man must first free himself from illusions and then work to attain another being. This work requires long and systematic efforts and knowledge.

Question. What is the difference between the school you speak of and the 'esoteric school' in the Theosophical Society? It seems to me that the idea underlying both is identical.

Ouspensky. The principal difference between the school of which I speak and the 'esoteric school' consists in the fact that the 'esoteric school' is, so to speak, the superstructure or the upper story of the whole theosophy. In order to come to the 'esoteric school' one must accept all the rest. And in the theosophical system there is very much that is naive, illogical, contradictory, and impossible.

Question. What is the difference between the 'Masters' and the beings of a higher mind?

Ouspensky. 'Masters' in theosophy, are connected with a definite *legend* which begins with Blavatsky. In accepting 'Masters' you have to accept the whole legend. Meanwhile there is very much that is unacceptable and impossible in this legend. *People of higher mind* are not connected with any sort of legend. Man as we know him is regarded not as the highest possible expression of his kind and not as a completed being but as a being in a certain definite phase of his possible *transformation.* This transformation is considered to be possible in one lifetime, that is, it is considered that a man born in one phase can, during one lifetime, pass into another. If we take the example of a butterfly then man is approximately a caterpillar. And the vast majority of people die as 'caterpillars'. But out of the masses of caterpillars a small percentage of transforming beings is constantly emerging. These evolving beings are, for us, *people of higher mind.* We can know of their existence by traces of their activity in history, chiefly in art and in religions. Possessing a more perfect mind than ordinary people they possess greater knowledge. The schools of which I speak have as their aim to bring ordinary people, who have felt or realized the necessity of escaping from their present state, near to the ideas coming from people of higher mind, because these ideas alone can assist their transformation, that is, their transition to a new level of being.

Question. Do you think that beings such as the Buddha or the Christ had 'school' knowledge?

Ouspensky. I cannot reply to the question about Christ and about Buddha because it must first be established what we accept and what we do not accept out of the legends connected with them. But if Christ really did exist then without doubt he taught his pupils *school science.*

The Gospels are full of references to a school system and to school knowledge.

Question. The idea of initiation in the 'esoteric school' is based on choice and appreciation of those who know better and that seems your idea too ('number of prepared people').

Ouspensky. The idea of initiation depending on someone else has absolutely no place in the system. Only self-initiation exists, that is, inner growth. Only *knowledge* can be received from someone else and it cannot be received in any other way. Preparation means something quite different. In its first sense it is simply intellectual and emotional preparation giving a man the possibility of understanding and *valuing* new ideas. The necessity of preparation is emphasized only to show that the ideas of the system cannot be given to everybody without discrimination. Of the fuller significance of *preparation* I will speak later.

Question. There are a great many people who claim to belong to a school and to possess special knowledge. All of them say what you are saying. Where is the criterion to be found by which we will recognize the right man? The examples of some of these people seem much more to deny their knowledge than to affirm it.

Ouspensky. Of course, besides real schools there exist many false schools. The chief danger comes from schools possessing a very small amount of knowledge and a very large amount of fantasy, such as the theosophical, anthroposphical, martinist and so on. It is very difficult to indicate an exact criterion for making a discrimination on first acquaintance with a school, because such a criterion depends on the depth and the quality of preparation. For me personally the first proof of *this* school being right was an undoubted and exact knowledge in psychology surpassing everything I had ever heard before anywhere, and making psychology an exact and practical science. This was a fact, for me incontrovertible, and I had a special preparation for judging this fact.

Schools can be of very different levels.

1 Preparatory schools of the fourth way can be divided into two categories. To the first category belong schools whose instructor acknowledges *the superiority of his own being over the being of the students* and by this promises the student help which is based on the use of powers which surpass the powers of ordinary man. And to the second category belong schools whose instructor acknowledges the superiority only *of his knowledge.*

2 Schools of the first category, that is, schools whose instructor acknowledges the superiority of his being and his possession of powers which ordinary man does not possess, are incommensurably more difficult and it is only possible to be in them by *constantly* remembering the principles of the work, by making a *complete* submission to the instructor and by *strictly* keeping the rules. The slightest deviation from remembering principles, from submitting to the instructor and from keeping rules makes continuing study in such a school impossible.

3 In schools of the second category the instructor can excuse many failings of individual students, even though it delays their work, so long as it does no harm to the general work of the school.

4 Making the difficulties of the work easier, reducing the demands or making concessions on the part of the instructor is never a privilege or an advantage for the students, on the contrary, it always indicates only failure of their work and their loss of place in the work.

5 Only raising or increasing the demands is a privilege.

6 Place in the work is determined by preparation, seniority, efforts, capacities, confidence in the instructor and understanding the aims of the work.

7 A student can begin without understanding fully the meaning of the ideas coming from higher mind and the aims of school work. But after a certain time a *right valuation* and understanding will be required of him and without this valuation and understanding he cannot continue.

8 The appearance of distrust towards the instructor and especially the expression of such distrust towards the knowledge, methods or personal opinions of the instructor makes continuing the work at the school impossible.

9 The student must remember that personal opinions of the instructor which contradict his own personal opinions are based on better methods of observation and reasoning than those which he can have at his disposal. For him, therefore, they should be a subject of study, not a subject of argument or objection.

10 He must remember that one of the aims of his work is a change in his points of view because his old points of view — being the points of view of a sleeping man — cannot be right. The task of the instructor is to show him the possibility of points of view which are in accord and which, at the same time, will contribute to his awakening.

11 The student must remember that he came to learn and not to teach or express his views.

12 Difference of opinion with the instructor can be an indication that the student has already obtained from him everything he can obtain and that he ought to leave the school and work independently. At the same time difference of opinion may simply show that the student has forgotten some of the fundamental principles of the work, or, what is still worse, has added something of his

own to it, something he did not hear from the instructor. This makes all further work useless.

13 Independent work outside the school is possible in contact with the instructor or without contact.

14 Contact depends on the student and not on the instructor and is established if the student remembers everything that he has at any time heard from the instructor and follows all of it without any kind of deviation, and above all without adding anything of his own.

15 The instructor bears the responsibility for the work of the students and can help them in their difficulties only when in relation to him, they follow the principles of schools of the first category and submit to the rules of schools in the first category; that is, when they never forget what has once been said to them and do not argue with the instructor.

16 This is sometimes called *imitating school work.*

17 In one and the same school there can be different students, that is, students of schools of the first category and students of schools of the second category. This difference between students is determined solely by their attitude towards the instructor.

NEW MODEL OF THE UNIVERSE
P.D. Ouspensky

Esoteric knowledge and psychological method are the underlying ideas of this encyclopaedic book. The wide range of subjects covered includes Christianity and the New Testament, systems of Yoga, Relativity, Space and Time, Dreams and Sex in its relation to the evolution of Man towards Superman.

1–85063–001–1

VIEWS FROM THE REAL WORLD
G.I. Gurdjieff

This collection of talks on the evolution of man is an authentic rendering of Gurdjieff's teaching, and demonstrates why he has come to be regarded as one of the most important spiritual masters of the twentieth century.

1–85063–002–X

MEETINGS WITH REMARKABLE MEN
G.I. Gurdjieff

In these colourful tales of adventure we are shown a completely
new way of facing life which touches us directly and gives us a
foretaste of another order of reality. *Meetings with Remarkable
Men* contains the only available information about the early life
of Gurdjieff.

1–85063–014–3

IN SEARCH OF THE MIRACULOUS
Fragments of an Unknown Teaching
P.D. Ouspensky

In Search of the Miraculous is written with the direct simplicity and honesty of all Ouspensky's books. Probably his best-known work, it is a vivid account of his three years' work with G.I. Gurdjieff from 1915 to 1918 under the difficult conditions of war and revolution. It describes Gurdjieff's cosmology from Ouspensky's perspective as a student, and shows how Ouspensky's formulation of his own ideas eventually led to his break with Gurdjieff. The book conveys a strong and lasting impression that not only did Ouspensky discover a real knowledge about Man and his relationship with the Universe, but that a practical cosmic teaching for the conduct of life is even now in existence.

This edition includes the Index previously published only separately.

'Undoubtedly a *tour de force*. To put entirely new and very complex cosmology and psychology into fewer than 400 pages, and to do this with a simplicity and vividness that makes the book accessible to any educated reader, is in itself something of an achievement.' *The Times Literary Supplement*.

0–7100–6635–X

STRANGE LIFE OF IVAN OSOKIN
P.D. Ouspensky

If you had the chance to live your life again, what would you do with it? P.D. Ouspensky's only novel, set in Moscow, on a country estate, and in Paris, tells what happened to Ivan Osokin when he was sent back twelve years to his stormy schooldays, early manhood and early loves.

First published in 1947, *Strange Life of Ivan Osokin* follows in the tradition of great Russian novels. It realises the theme of 'eternal recurrence', a theory of time developed in Ouspensky's *New Model of the Universe* (ARKANA 1984). The novel was described by the *Manchester Guardian* as 'a brilliant fantasy . . . written to illustrate the theme that we do not live life but that life lives us.'

1–85063–083–6